BUILDING UP OF THE NUMBERS

God's Fingerprint

JAMES L. ANDERSON

WESTBOW® PRESS
A DIVISION OF THOMAS NELSON
& ZONDERVAN

WestBow Press books may be ordered through booksellers or by contacting:

WestBow Press
A Division of Thomas Nelson
1663 Liberty Drive
Bloomington, IN 47403
www.westbowpress.com
1 (866) 928-1240

ISBN: 978-1-4908-1879-5 (sc)
ISBN: 978-1-4908-2011-8 (hc)
ISBN: 978-1-4908-1880-1 (e)

Library of Congress Control Number: 2013922948

Printed in the United States of America.

WestBow Press rev. date: 01/08/2014

Contents

Acknowledgments

Thanks to all my loved ones who were there when I was too little and too sick. I thank my grandmother, Caroline Anderson, who passed away in 1975. Without her, there wouldn't have been a way out. I thank her for her strength and determination and, above all, her warm and loving arms.

Thanks to my Aunt Gladys who passed away a few years ago. She was always a source of provision and love, and she is greatly missed. Thanks to Aunt Mag, who was there when everyone else left town. Thanks to Aunt Joyce. When I came to New Mexico, she welcomed me with open arms.

Thanks to Joshua Johnson who brought my mother to pick me up and take me back to California, who tried to give me advice and who advised me to go to Las Vegas. Joshua passed away two years ago and has been greatly missed. Thanks to his sister, O. Brown and her family who were always cousins to me.

Thanks to the Moore family: Brother Moore and Mother Moore have always been more than cousins to me. Thanks to Pluck: oh, what a friend! Thanks to the Morgan family who offered their home to me.

Thanks to my dear mother, Jean. She was not there when I was young, for she was young herself. But later in life, the Lord knew that she wanted to make a difference in my life, and she did. When I went through a divorce, she was there with words of encouragement and finances.

Thanks to my wonderful wife, Pat, whom the Lord sent to me. She was and is always there for me. I thank her for her encouragement and support. Besides Jesus and the heavenly Father, she is the love of my life.

Introduction

When I first came to Christ, I recognized his peace and his sweet sleep (Ps. 4:8). He was the Spirit to belong to, someone and something special. As I grew closer to the Lord, I began to recognize His ways and attributes and who he was. I began to experience his faithfulness, patience, forgiveness, authority (Deut. 1:17), omniscience (Ps. 147:4), justice, righteousness, *agape* love, sovereignty, and grace. As I grew and matured in his Word, I also noticed that God is a God of order (Ps. 50:21). Nothing takes God by surprise. His plan, His will, and His purpose are outside of time (1 Peter 1:18–20). Everything that happens regarding salvation, the rapture and resurrection, and the second coming was prepared outside of time.

God judges and executes in His perfect time. He is a fair and righteous God, all-knowing (omniscient), all-powerful (omnipotent), and everywhere (omnipresent) (Isa. 40:12–15; 45:5–7). He chastens those whom He loves (Heb. 12:6). He does not answer our prayers according to our will but according to His will (Isa. 1:15).

As I began to observe the Holy Spirit (Ps. 25:4), I said, "Show me your ways, O Lord. He began to show me His numbers for my life: one (1) through thirteen (13) and other numbers, as well as twenty-three (23), which seemed to be my number. Number 5 is the number of grace. Number 7 is God's number of totality, perfection, completeness, and universality. The number 12 is God's government. You get the idea. There are other ways to come to these numbers. For instance, Thursday is the fifth day of the week, and October is the tenth (10) month.

These numbers have been in my life, and they have a story to tell.

CHAPTER 1

Highway 35: The Beginning

I was born off Highway 35, which was where a lot of things took place in my life. My mother was only fourteen when she was pregnant with me. It didn't start out right from the very beginning. My mother was bitten by a snake in the outhouse while she was pregnant with me, which was a terrible thing.

The numbers in my mother's birthday were the year thirty-three (33), which is the victory number twice (Luke 2:46; Matt. 27:63) however, three (3) is also the number of conclusion, There was more conclusions than victories. The month of October, the tenth month, which is the number for perfection and completion in the Bible (Matt. 25:28), and day five (5), which is the number for grace (Gen. 15:9; Rev. 9:5–6). In retrospect, my mother had the numbers of victory, conclusion, completeness, perfection, and grace.

As I recall, we were very poor but happy. We lived in the poorest state in the union, in Forest, Mississippi.

1

In retrospect, God was always there. There were times when my cousin and I, along with other neighborhood children, almost drowned in the many ponds and creeks. When my grandmother came looking for us, we could always hear her calling in the distance. She knew we were doing something we should not have been doing, like swimming in someone's pond. She had reason to be worried, for one of our schoolmates drowned. We had some close calls, but thank God that by His grace nothing bad ever happened.

My grandmother took us to a church called Mars' Hill (Acts 17:22). It was right next to Highway 35. There were times during the summer months when, after a service, everyone brought food, and we got under the shade trees and had a picnic. We needed the fellowship and spiritual food as well, for life was not easy at times.

One very rainy night, two of my aunts and a male friend of theirs were traveling home from a visit to my grandmother's house. I was staying with them for a few days during the summer and we were headed to their house in the truck, as we prepared to stop and turn left, the pickup truck was hit from behind. My aunt and I sat in the middle and I was fast asleep in her lap when we were hit. To this day, I don't know how I ended up under the truck in a puddle of water. Other than being wet, skinned-up, and shaken-up, I was okay on the outside, but on the inside it was a different matter. I had a pebble in my right ear that stayed there for many years before it disappeared. The nightmares were the worst. I don't know how long it lasted, but again I thanked God for his grace.

My aunties talked for a long time about the weird way that I ended up under the truck.

Life was not easy off Highway 35. My father was murdered when I was about four. I was born out of wedlock, so I didn't know him and never saw him alive or dead. Years later, I got a picture of him in the army. As a child, I heard others describe how he had been murdered. Many years later, I came back to town, and as we passed the old house by the railroad tracks where we'd once lived, someone pointed out to me the man who had murdered my father.

Life is so strange, so unpredictable. This man did twenty years in prison—and then renovated the very house we'd once lived in. I was thinking the other day that if I had that same opportunity again, I would approach him and ask him if he knew Jesus.

A Shortcut off Highway 35

Highway 35 had a lot of grace in it for the things we went through. The last bad thing that happened off 35 was when I accompanied my cousins, we were coming back from the store. We had decided to take a shortcut off the main dirt road. As we went through the woods, we saw two guys standing there. As we passed them, they grabbed our cousin and threw her to the ground. We ran home and told what had happened to her. Nothing was ever done about it.

The number 35 represents victory (3) and grace (5). After three (3) days of searching, Mary and Joseph found young Jesus in the temple. The two spies abode in Jericho for three (3) days, and the pursuers found them, not (Josh. 2:22). The number five (5) is grace (Rev. 9:5–6). Thank God for his wonderful grace. William is a biblical scholar and author says," The covenant is founded on grace, for five (5) living creatures were sacrificed to establish it (Gen. 15:9)."

Elohim: this is a plural word meaning *Gods*. This is the name that gives us the Trinity, three (3) Gods in one. We can also say that we get our victory in three (3) God the Father, God the Son, and God the Holy Spirit. As I went forward, I would see His numbers in my life. I believe this to be the foundation of my life.

Highway 80, Highway 21

When I was about nine, I moved into town with my mother and aunts. We lived across the railroad tracks. There was a large cesspool about four blocks behind the house in the wooded area. Sometimes it had a smell to it. They often had to put something in it to help eliminate the smell. The house was a shack. On one side of the front porch, you had to be very careful or you would literally fall through. When it rained, we would go running for buckets for all the leaks in the roof of the house. I will never forget how much the monthly rent was, every month my mother and her sisters had a hard time raising it. Three (3) big dollars, and we are not talking about victory, but the conclusion of the matter.

One day I went to the neighborhood store, and the owner asked me if I wanted a job. I didn't ask how much he was paying, but I thought *it's a job*. He asked me if I had sticky hands. I didn't know what he was talking about, but I knew my hands didn't have anything sticky on them. He said he would give me a certain amount of pay, plus all the food I could eat. That was a mistake.

Looking back, God took care of the fatherless and poor. He also took care of the righteous through Jesus. I worked there off and on for about four years. After a while, I wanted a raise. I knew how to scrape up a few dollars, so there were times when I didn't go to work at the store. But I was a good worker. I sacrificed many summers working at the store. Even at that age, I knew I could never save anything working there. He never gave me a raise, but he never said anything about how much I ate.

Highway 80 passed on the right side of the store. Eight (8) is the number of new beginnings, according to Genesis 8:18. Noah and his family of eight (8) started the new world. This was my starter job. Years later, when I came back to town, I got other jobs on Highway 80.

Highway 21 correlates with the number for the Trinity or, you could say, three sevens (7). In Revelation 5:12 and 7:11–12, God grants his sevenfold blessing, which is God's number of completeness, totality, perfection, and universality.

Notice all the sevens in these verses, where Jacob spoke of the tribe of Judah from which Jesus would come. The Lord told David, who was of the tribe of Judah, that it was his family through which the Messiah would come (2 Sam. 7). It is ironic that in 1 Samuel 7, after a great victory over the Philistines, the prophet Samuel erected a stone between Mizpah and Shen and called it *Ebenezer* (1 Sam. 7:12), which means "the stone of help." In 2 Samuel 7:12, God said, "And when your days be fulfilled, and you shall sleep with your fathers, I will set up your seed after you, which shall proceed out of your bowels, and I will establish his kingdom." This speaks of Christ. It then says, "He shall build a house for my name, and I will establish the throne of his kingdom forever" (2 Sam. 7:13). This means that the stone of help is actually Christ. What was illustrated in 1 Samuel 7:12, was promised in 2 Samuel 7:12.

In Isaiah 7:12 we're told how this would happen: "Behold, a virgin shall conceive, and bear a son, and shall call his name Emmanuel." Also, in Isaiah 53:7 we're told the manner in which redemption would be brought about, which was the cross. The verse says that he was oppressed, and he was afflicted, yet he opened not his mouth. He was brought as a lamb to the slaughter. God's chapters and verses are all represented here as sevens. We serve an awesome God!

God put on my heart at the age of fourteen to start saving my money, because he had plans for my life. I cared nothing about the small town I lived in. It did not have much to offer—no opportunities, no hope, nothing for a young person at that time. I knew there was something bigger and better than the life that I was living or hoped for.

My grandfather on my mother's side died when I was only eight (8), which was the beginning number. There were almost no men in my life, not to mention the things that came with being poor. For instance, shame and fear come with being poor—fear of not having any clothes or shoes to wear, or food to eat. When I saw classmates who lived on the other side of town come through my neighborhood, I ran and hid, hoping they didn't see me. However, I never knew when God would give me an opportunity to leave Forest. I worked and saved my money, when the time came I was ready to leave.

My uncle came home for some reason, but he would soon return to New Mexico, and I said that I wanted to go with him. My aunt said I shouldn't go, but I said I had my own money and that I was going. Besides, I was the only one of my immediate family who had not left. My mother had left to seek opportunity, along with everyone else, leaving me with the only aunt who was left. But God had a reason for that. When Auntie Mag's only child was ready to be born, I had to run through a cold, snowy winter morning to get the midwife.

After saving every dime from my job, my turn came to leave. I didn't know how much a ticket was, because I didn't know where I was going. But God had put in my heart how much to save. God is always good! This was the first Time I had left Mississippi. It was a victory to me thru the third (3) month march (Lk.2:46). Four (4) months after President Kennedy was assassinated. The number four (4) is the number of completeness in creation (Eze.1: 10). The next nine (9) years, the number nine (9) was His fourfold grace that protected me (matt.27:45-46; 50). I was all over the West. God was teaching me the things I needed to know and giving me an experience.

His divine providence was always there. When I was nineteen, I took some drugs—LSD or "acid." I almost lost my mind. I had a spiritual experience with Jesus and the Devil. I remember that a person came to my bed in the hospital and he had the face of some kind of scary spirit. I could only see him while I was on drugs. The fear of seeing this evil person caused me to run into the hallway with only my gown on. The hallway was full of people. I could only see images of the Lord through the lights, but I could hear and discern His words of encouragement. If my memory serves me right, it was a Sunday—resurrection Sunday. You could call it the eighth day, as it would be the beginning of that part of my life.

The Lord also told me to some degree that my life was not in order, or something to that effect. He said that I must get my life in order. However I came back home many more times, each time with a different experience, having been cut up, shot at, and put in jail.

There was a time when I had gotten a job on Highway 80 with the horse show, and the job was about to end. The show had another engagement in Louisiana, so I decided to go as far west as they were going. I left for the bus station right away, only to find out that I was short on the bus fare! It was too late to change my mind, so I went to the highway. It was my first time hitchhiking, but I had no other choice.

It wasn't long before an eighteen (18) wheeler came along—eighteen being the number of beginning (Gen. 8:18). It took me all the way to Dallas, Texas, where I could then afford to purchase a ticket for my destination. I came back home once more for the last time, only to work for a short period of time. Then I went back to California. God had used four (4) states to prepare me for the fifth (5) state.

I worked in Palm Springs as a busboy, hitchhiking to and from work. My mother lived in Banning, California, only twenty-two miles away. After saving my money I bought another car. Once again, the Lord rewarded me for my determination.

Time was running out, and I knew it. A nice, old Jewish couple always gave me a job each time I came into town, broke and hungry, but that was coming to an end. Mr. Marvin Weiss came to me one day and said he had heard I was going to Vegas. I told him I was thinking about it. He told me there was plenty of work in Vegas and that this would be my last job working for him. He didn't tell me the reason why. He had always liked my work. But as I look back, I see that God was closing that door as well. A few years later, I would learn that they had sold the place.

After having my last spiritual experience in May, God's grace was leading me to Las Vegas (Jesus' five names [Isa. 9:6] and fivefold ministry [Eph. 4:11]). To this day, I don't understand everything that transpired that night. I remember waking up and saying, "What have I been doing with my life? I'm wasting time." It was a new day. The sky never been as blue or the trees greener, and the singing of the birds had never been prettier than that day! A friend of my mother's, whom I had known since I was a kid, said, "Jimmy, go to Las Vegas and do something with your life." There is nothing here for a young man. I took his advice, because the Lord had closed all the doors in every state where I'd been. It was God's grace that would take me to the unknown.

Las Vegas

I came to Las Vegas on the twenty-third (23) day of the seventh month of 1973. I was twenty-four (4) years old. Four (4) was the complete number of creation (Gen. 13:14). God had made me complete in my trials. The twenty-third (23) is my birthday and an important day in my life. I was also baptized on that day, which was in the fifth (5) month—yes, the month of grace—which means that I was identified with Christ on that day. One number twenty-three (23) was physical and one was spiritual, and there would be many other twenty-threes. The seventh (7) month is God's number, and this would be a very important number in my life. I came to Vegas in the year seventy-three (73). Seven (7) was God's perfect timing in my life, and three (3) would be the conclusion of it

What did these numbers represent in my life at this point? When broken down, the first number in twenty-three (2) means "witness" in the Bible. Of course, each number has a reference to the Bible. It is not always as a whole number (as in twenty-three (23), but sometimes you need to separate the numbers. *Two* represents "witnesses" (Rev. 11:3). *Three* (3) is God's number of victory. After three (3) days, Jesus rose from the dead (Matt. 27:63).

Later in the book we will see that my wife and I were called, or prophesied, to be two (2) of God's witnesses. We know that God's number is seven (7) (Gen. 2:2). All creation was complete and perfect, and He rested on the seventh (7) day. So, what was God saying in *my* numbers? He was saying that He would make my wife and I witness the victory in our lives.

I went to Vegas, and after about two weeks, I started to work at the Dunes Hotel. Now God's numbers were all over the place, but we want take notice of every number, or we would never finish the book. I worked at the Dunes Hotel washing dishes, or "pearl diving," as we called it. At that time in my life, I had done all kinds of work, and I was proud of that. The Lord said, "Do not hate small beginnings" (Zech. 4:10). I worked there for about a year before realizing that it was a dead-end job. I went back to the union hall, and the lady told me that MGM was hiring across the street and was promoting bus persons to waiters.

I said I would take a chance. At that time, I didn't know the Lord as I do now. At the same time, I knew that he had always been there. I started out as a runner. That meant keeping the restaurant dining room stocked with dishes and other supplies. I did that for about two weeks before a position opened for a bus person. I worked as a waiter when they were short of help. After six months, I was promoted to waiter. The room I worked in was a coffee shop. However, there was room to move up to a top restaurant. The advantages were there at that time.

The MGM was the most famous hotel on the strip in Las Vegas—other than the Hilton and Caesar's Palace, which were at the top. There were always stars coming into the coffee shop for a quick bite to eat. There was a maître d' who worked next door in the famous Barrymore Room, named after the Barrymore family: John, Ethel, and Lionel. When the maître d' came over to the coffee shop, I always asked for a job in his room. He was always in a hurry.

Finally, there was an opening, but they weren't hiring. They were using the extras. After a period of time, the Lord allowed a new food and beverage company to take over the hotel. God gave me favor with the manager, and he made an opening for me. When the time came, I got cold feet and told him to give the job to someone else. I said I would wait for the next position. But the manager said I would have to take the job because I had more seniority. Satan was trying to scare me and he did!

But God had given me that job, and his fingerprints (numbers) were on it. In the year seventy-seven (77), I went into the room after twenty-seven (27) months, indicating that I would witness God. Also, the numbers were saying that it was by the will of the Father through the Son. God was always there.

In 1975 my grandmother passed away at the age of seventy-five (75). Born in 1900 (19), she was a very sweet woman. In looking at her numbers the year she passed away, I saw that she had died in the same month in which she had been born August, the month of beginning. She had been in my life for a number of reasons, thank God, but most importantly, she had ensured that I went to school. She was the reason I got the basics of education. Without her, that wouldn't have been possible. Her numbers was God's grace in my life. The number nine (9) being the number of God's fourfold grace. It is a number that must be separated. That makes it fourfold grace. If we look at (Matt. 27: 45-46; 50, it shows us His number nine in both verses. It shows us, Jesus was full of Grace and Truth. Verse (50) shows us after he died, we will receive His dispensation of grace, His fourfold grace. What is also interesting is the 'nine (9) gifts of the Holy Spirit", (1 Cor. 12:8-10). The Spirit of grace thru Christ's instructions, relative to who gets what. We also have the 'nine (9) fruit of the Spirit "as well (Gal. 5:22).

God gave me an experience with one of the most important characteristics: *wisdom*. The Hebrew word is *chokhmah*, which means knowledge, experience, insight, intelligence, and judgment. It is always used in a positive sense. True wisdom leads to the reverence for the Lord (Job 28:28; Prov. 2:2). *Chokhmah* is used to describe an entire range of human experiences (Ex. 28:3). God is all-powerful and all-knowing. Therefore, all wisdom has its source with him (Job 11:6; Prov. 11:2. The gray hair of experience is the splendor of the old Prov. 20:29b.

The time came in my life when I had to make a change. Being in Vegas gave me plenty of time and opportunity to be on the party scene, which I didn't need. At the same time, I took care of business. I moved out of one house to an upgraded one. The numbers on that house were 1225.

The number twelve (12) refers to God's government. At age twelve, Jesus said, "I must be about my Father's business" (Luke 2:49). There are twelve (12) gates (Rev. 21:12) and twelve (12) apostles (Rev. 21:14). The number two (2) refers to God's witness, and five (5) is God's grace. National Prayer Day is the first Thursday of May, which is the fifth (5) day of the fifth (5) month.

In this house numbered 1225, I would accept the Lord, according to Romans 10:9 –10. Praise God! Israel became a nation in the month of May, and the year was 1948. I was also born in 1948. The number four (4) is fourfold, complete number of creation. It is the number of the earth and its four (4) seasons: spring, summer, fall, and winter. There are four (4) directions (Gen.13:14), four (4) winds of heaven (Zech. 4:6). We also have the four (4) Gospels. God's numbers are part of His nature. As we look at (John 11:17), Lazarus has been in the grave for (4) days. It is interesting to note: why four (4) days? Why not one (1), or two (2), or even three (3)? I believe, because the number four (4) is the complete number of creation

(Eze.1:10). As we see His numbers in the earlier part of the book regarding (1 Sam. and 2 Sam.), speaking of all the sevens (7). His numbers are a part of Him.

As I was saying earlier, time would change at this point in my life. My lifestyle was catching up with me. One day as I was going to the mailbox in front of the house, I heard a bang. I thought a car had backfired. At the same time, a bullet sung past my head, and I realized what had just transpired. I don't know if the bullet was meant for me or someone else. Again, I thank God for His number five (5) on my home address of grace.

I remember getting caught up in horoscopes, which is what happens when you leave Christ out, when you have a spiritual void. I remember sending off for an astrological forecast. I remember having nightmares and not being able to wake up. I dreamed of being buried alive, six feet under. I dreamed of terrible-looking animals. Thank the Lord Jesus that he knew my heart, because Jesus knows the heart of man. However, the Bible does not teach *unconditional* eternal security, only eternal security (Heb. 3:6, 14). The Holy Spirit will not stay where he is not welcome or in an environment where he gets grieved day in and day out. Only God knows when that time comes.

A woman came to the restaurant one day, and the maître d' told me that she could read palms. Well, she could only go so far as to tell me that I had a gift. She asked me what it was, and I told her I didn't know. Perhaps it was a gift that the Lord gave me. When I finally received my astrological forecast, I was very excited. When I opened it, it said that on a certain day all these great things were going to happen. The date was November 21, 1980. Keep these numbers in mind.

We celebrated the night before my "lucky" day. The next morning, my first wife at the time called me at home to tell me that the MGM was on fire. I accused her of playing a joke on me. She said to look out the window. There was smoke everywhere. We were laid off for eight (8) months. The numbers were the same as the two highways back in the South, Highways 21 and 80, which were the numbers of beginning. The number twenty one (21) represents The Trinity. God was saying, "Only I am all-knowing" (Ps. 147:4). With the number eight (8), God had my attention. I knew all along that this horoscope business about my future was a joke, because I was now laughing. During the eight (8) months that I was out of work, there were no other jobs. The hotel employed four thousand people full-time and another thousand part-time, which was five (5) thousand total. I had worked for about six (6) weeks on another job, before getting laid off, which is man's number (Rev. 13:18). I had a long way to go before the reopening of the hotel. I would test the numbers, for eight (8) was a beginning of something. Thank God I had the number five (5) the grace number!

Surviving the Fire for the Next Six and a Half Months

After being laid off for almost two months, money was running out fast. I had purchased a new car, which came with a payment. I'll talk more about the car in a moment. I had a mortgage and two kids at that time, and I still had not knowingly accepted the Lord. Nevertheless, he was always there. In retrospect, I knew I'd received Him as a child. I just needed to confess (1 John 1:9). Even after salvation a person repeats the salvation prayer many times. My car payment was $300 (3) per month, which is God's victory number (Matt. 27:45).

There was darkness over all the land, from the sixth hour to the ninth (9) hour. After three (3) hours, Jesus gave up his spirit. Victory not for him but for us. It was the ninth (9) hour, three (3) p.m., when he gave up his spirit, and that gave us the victory. Also the ninth (9) represents- God's fourfold grace. (Matt. 27:45-46; 50

I went to the dealership that had control of my car payment at that time. They said they would only charge me for the interest for six months. Six (6) is the number of man (Rev. 13:18). The car was a 1978 Cadillac Seville, a light lemon-yellow color, perfect for the desert temperatures in Las Vegas. The number seven (7) is God's number, and eight (8) is the number of new beginnings. Those numbers would turn out to be exactly what they represented: God's number of perfection, totality, and completeness.

On the eighth (8) day, Jesus became the first fruits of the resurrection (1 Cor. 15:20). This car would be the beginning of a long relationship. What do I mean by that?

Well, I went through the fire at the hotel, two job strikes, and a divorce that was God's will. Someone said, "If God sends them away, don't go chasing after them." Someone else said, "The reason divorce is so expensive is because it's worth it. At the same time, God hates divorce, and everyone, including the children, suffers.

My license plate number is 556BNC. In one sentence, this would mean: "God's double grace for me, before not Christ like." Exodus 14:8 says "that the children of Israel went out with a high hand." Were they high-fiving, or what? Yad is the Hebrew word for hand, power, and strength (Ex. 14:8). Can mean a mighty hand from God. It is interesting to note: mighty hand which can be a metaphor for grace. A hand has five (5) fingers which is the number of grace. Each person's hands or fingerprints are different, as God's hands and fingerprints are different than ours and means so much more. God told me five (5) things in a dream some time ago. I couldn't remember the last one, because I'd been too lazy to get out of bed to write it down. Now the Lord was saying, *"How bad do you want it"?* Years later, it came to me by a word from the Lord: "There is five (5); one is in your hand." The grace and sovereignty of God and his signs and wonders amaze me! I only worked for six (6) weeks, but, praise God, I was able to get a loan on my home, which enabled me to take it easy for a period of time until I went back to work. Again, God was good, but I still did not have a relationship with Him.

When we went back to work, we got new lockers for our personal belongings. One day when I opened my locker, I found a simple piece of brown paper. What was written on it was almost scary: the number 237. To this day I don't know how it got in my locker. When "my" number (twenty-three (23) is combined with God's number (seven (7)), it changes everything. I still have that simple, brown paper. It was nothing fancy but was straight to the point—just as Jesus would be. I did redraw the numbers, because they faded over time.

The Lord gave me the title of this book," *Building Up of the Numbers*". It means exactly what it says. As I continued to observe the numbers, I continued to be amazed at all the places they were. Even as I write, I notice numbers that I didn't know were there.

On my father's side of the family, there was sclerosis of the liver, which affected only the men. My father's brothers all died in their fifties from that disease. My grandfather died young as well, I don't know what from. It didn't happen to my daddy, but in a sense, it killed him. He had gone over to my grandmother's house after having too much to drink. His younger brother had gotten into an argument with my grandmother's boyfriend. She had put my father to bed, unaware of the argument that had taken place. When this maniac came in with a double-bladed ax, he mistook my daddy for my uncle and killed my daddy. Because of that horrible act, there was a closed casket.

These things stayed in my mind for a long time. When the doctor discovered symptoms of the disease in me, it refreshed the terrible memories of my childhood. I had been told or had heard other adults talking about how awful it was. My father had his own cleaning and laundry business. Before that he had served in the army. It was the alcohol that he couldn't control. Years later, God would show me in a dream a glass of rum that I was drinking. The ice cubes were little demon spirits. That was the last time I drank rum.

I realized that my daddy and uncles hadn't had must of a chance. A person just cannot stop drinking unless he changes his lifestyle. Jesus' finished work on the cross is the only way to do that. People go through rehabilitation programs with small success. They just replace the alcohol with three packs of cigarettes and sixteen cups of coffee a day. All the time worried about falling off the wagon. A Christian can have problems as well. The apostle Paul dealt with the sins of the flesh (Rom. 7:15–24). At that time, he didn't understand the prescribed order of victory. Even today, most churches don't understand the prescribed order of victory.

Paul was a new person in Christ, baptized and filled with the Holy Spirit. He as well as most of the church today, thought that he had the power to will sin from his life. In Romans 7:25, the Lord revealed to Paul that no one had the answer to that problem, not even the inner circle, Peter, James, or John. That revelation was given to the apostle Paul. My pastor said, "No matter how much you go to church or get involved with activities or fasting and prayer, they won't solve the problem." All those things are good, but we must not let those things become works, for we are to rest in the Lord.

We must walk in the spirit, not in the flesh (Rom. 8:1–2). The work is finished. We live and have faith in Jesus finished work on the cross—the cross being the means and Jesus being the source. We are sanctified and positioned in Him. We are under the dispensation of grace, not the law. "Not by power, nor by might, but by my spirit," said the Lord (Zech. 4:6). I realized that drugs and alcohol and my current lifestyle were too strong for me.

Some years later, I would find the victory that is in the cross. I would ask in faith and wait. You see, it's not *how much* faith a person has that matters, for faith the size of a mustard seed will move mountains. It's the *object* of one's faith that matters: Jesus and his sacrifice on the cross. You cannot separate them.

One day, after purchasing a satellite dish and changing my friends, I was watching satellite TV and came upon a pastor. I made it a habit to watch him five (5) days a week. I watched others as well. Finally, after no drinking, I regained a clear mind. When the pastor offered up a salvation prayer, I accepted the Lord Jesus Christ. I was thirty-seven (37) at that time, and God's numbers were there.

His grace was evident in the *five (5)* days a week that I watched the pastor. My age contained a *three (3)* and a *seven (7)*. *Three (3)* is the victory number. Mark 14:41 says that Jesus went three times to the Father to determine that the cross was the will of the Father, that was victory for us. Revelation 7:12 talks of God's *seven*fold blessing. Jesus told Paul in (2 Cor. 12:9) after Paul asked the Lord to take the thorn in the flesh away, "My grace is sufficient for thee." When he was weak, he was strong this was victory for Paul.

I didn't understand the total message of the gospel at the time, but I knew it was all about trust. My faith would grow and develop in time. Paul said in 2 Corinthians 5:17, "Therefore, if anyone is in Christ, he is a new creation; old things have passed away; behold, all things have become new." I began to notice the difference in myself. I wanted a place to belong, a church similar to the ones on TV, but I found none.

One day a guy came by the house with some pamphlets. He asked if he could come by and study with me the next week. Later, he invited me to come to the "hall," as he called it. Finally, I went to the hall. I went two times before I noticed that there were no windows or excitement. In retrospect, I realized that there was no Holy Spirit. Later, someone told me that it was the meeting place for Jehovah's Witnesses. At that time, I didn't know anything about them, but I left there and never went back. The first church doesn't mean your last church, but it could mean that it is God's will at that time. My first church although I was not there long, I had a baptism experience.Pastor House baptized me. As I came out of the water, I felt as if I was walking on air. You can say, it felt as if I was on drugs of some kind, except it was pure and natural. When I said the salvation prayer I had no experience of this kind, but at this time I was instructed to go and be baptized. Obedience brings blessings, I needed that experience at that time.

I read an article in a commentary by Jimmy Swaggart. He talked about A. N. Trotter, who had been a missionary and evangelist many years ago. Trotter told of one of his experiences in Africa. He spoke of an African who had been seeking the Lord, asking for God to reveal himself to him. Having been raised in witchcraft, the man had no true knowledge of God. He had never heard a gospel message or attended a gospel service. But in his heart, he knew there was a God, and he also knew that he did not know him. The African man sought the Lord for some days. An angel suddenly appeared unto him and told him to go to the coast and travel north. The man immediately followed the instructions of the angel and proceeded to run to the coastline of West Africa and then go north. He went well over one hundred miles.

As he followed the coastline, he came to several villages. He stopped at each village, but each time, the angel appeared and instructed him to keep moving. This went on for several days, until he finally came to the outskirts of Monrovia, Liberia, West Africa. Upon arriving in the city, he saw a church. He had never been to church, but he knew enough about it to know that a church was where one was supposed to be able to learn about God. He proceeded to enter, but the angel appeared again and said, "No! This is not the place. Keep going!" The exact same thing happened several times, with the angel intervening each time. Finally, not by accident but having been led by the Lord, he came to the church where Brother Trotter was the pastor.

Because the angel had stopped him several times already, he now hesitated before the front door. The angel appeared again and said, "This is the one. Go in." It was a Sunday morning, and the people were in the midst of a service. Because the angel had finally told him that this was the place where he could find God, he became so overjoyed that he burst through the front door and created quite a scene, which interrupted the service. The deacons, who did not understand the reason for his obvious joy, started to restrain him. However, Brother Trotter sensed the presence of the Lord and finally found someone who could speak the man's language and find out his story.

In a few minutes, the man made Jesus his Savior. A few hours later, maybe even at the same service, he was baptized with the Holy Spirit, evidenced by his speaking in other tongues (Acts 2:4). The man wanted to go back to his village immediately and tell the story of what the Lord had done for him. However, Brother Trotter persuaded him to stay for several months and enter the Bible school that was associated with the church. This he did, and then he went back to his own village. He became one of the greatest preachers of the gospel in that part of Africa. Thousands of people were won to Christ through his ministry.

From this story, I was struck with the importance of getting "church" right the first time. Or perhaps ascertaining being in His will. I didn't find the church that I was looking for, but I continued to watch certain ministries on TV, reading along in my first Bible, which I had purchased. Finally, after a period of *two (2)* years (God's number of witness), the Lord had taken away the drugs and I felt like I had grown spiritually. A few years after that, I found a church that I would attend for about *three (3)* years. I received the victory in the number three (3) when I discovered my gifts.

My new wife and I joined the church and attended there together. She was a member of another church before we met. Earlier, I had also joined a church—the first church that I had attended—for a short period of time. It was August, the month of beginning (Luke 24:1–6). Jesus rose on Sunday, which is the eighth (8) day on the calendar and is called the Lord's Day. After some time and some spiritual growth—after growing in his grace, love, and faith—I decided to test my faith and trust God. The year was 1988, the year of beginning, or in this case, a *double* beginning! God knows when to make the first move. My pastor always said, "Don't get ahead of God." I knew an employee at work who was building his first home, and he invited me to come by and take a look at the progress. After I looked at his house, my acquaintance told me how to go about the process for myself. The Lord gave me the faith to pursue this project. After buying magazines that had pictures of houses, square footage, and floor plans, I made a choice on the house and the layout and started to look for land. These were exciting times! After finding the land, I would have to pay it off, find subcontractors, and get a construction loan. I had gotten all the advice I thought I needed. I had read all the books. It was now time for the land!

First things first: we had a baby girl, born on January 10, 1988. *Ten (10)* is the number of completion in the Bible. In some cases, it means "perfection" (Matt. 25:19-20; 1 Sam. 25:38; Gen. 28:22. This was the last child I would father; hence it was the number of completion.

I started to look for land, but I didn't like the location. One day my x-wife and I were driving and looking, when she said, "Why don't we look for land on the other side of town in another neighborhood?" I had already looked in that area, but I didn't think she would like it.

We finally found a vacant lot that was close to an acre of land and had a "for sale" sign on it. We decided to make a call and see how the process worked. An elderly lady came out and told us to make an offer.

CHAPTER 2

The Land Deal of the Century

"I don't believe it! I *can't* believe it!" The elderly woman's voice screamed out of the phone. I remember asking, "Can't believe what?" She finally made her point. She said the price of the land was $25,000. Someone had offered $24,500, and she had rejected it. Another person had made an offer for $24,000, and she had rejected it. She said, "Then you come along and make an offer for $19,500!"

She accepted it! Hallelujah! Praise God! I don't totally remember my reply, but I remember saying something about faith.

I got a copy of a map at city hall, which showed our purchase as lot number *eight (8)*, the number of new beginning (Gen. 7:13). The lot was a virgin lot, which means that God had made sure that I was the one for that land. Also, the Lord was saying that when He has something for you, no one can take it from you. The land was centrally located. We could walk downtown, and according to the mileage on my car, it was eight (8) miles from the strip.

The number fifty-five (55) hundred (the amount of money I saved) off the original price typifies God's grace, which is *five (5)*. I woke up one morning saying, "I was once blind, but now I see. It's amazing grace!" (John 9:25). A few years later, Dr. Gary L. Greenwald—world-renowned prophet, evangelist, and pastor—foretold that I would see and understand the Scriptures, along with other things, and this has been true. It took me *fifteen (15)* months to pay off the land, which was by God's grace. As I put my attention back on my job, God had me focus on being more Christ like and continuing to grow in Him. During my job as a server, the pastor told my wife and I that we were "double servers." We served the public as waiter and waitress as well as serving at our church. At that time, our employer gave us the opportunity to become "employee of the month," with the chance of being "employee of the year." This gave us the incentive to bring out our best.

I put my best foot forward to get employee of the month, which was awarded to one person each month from each of *four (4)* departments. I was the employee of the month in our restaurant, and there was a total of *forty-eight (48)* employees in the contest for the year. My résumé included top seniority, many letters of appreciation, letters of acknowledgement of expertise, and turning in a $500 gambling chip (which was written down for my credit).

I'd had no write-ups, and I'd worked for *seven* (7) years without calling in sick. The number seven (7) is God's number for totality and completion. I was not perfect, but in this case, no one could beat me but myself!

A Dream of Humility

Some years before or after, I don't remember I had a dream. In this vivid dream I saw a woman's face, her skin color, and her personality. She had a sweet spirit of humility. I told her that I was getting ready to go back to the place I'd come from, and I asked her to pack my bags. She came back with this little brown bag and said, "This is all you have." Notice that the bag was brown, just like the paper with the number that I'd found earlier in my locker. A brown bag is itself indicative of humility. I will never forget the sweet tone of her voice as she said, "This is all you have."

I responded by saying, "Where I'm from, I have a big house, a *three (3)*-car garage (victory), and many cars." In my dream, I was currently in a place that I sensed was in Texas. I was *twenty-three* (23) at the time. The number twenty-three (23) isn't always friendly; sometimes it indicates a bittersweet experience. But then, wisdom can be bittersweet. It's part of gaining wisdom.

As I was getting ready to leave, I noticed how dark and lonely that place was. When I left, I thought about how blessed I was, considering what I was leaving behind and what I was going back to. It gave me a sense of the finished work of the Lord, for he was humble in spirit and in nature (Matt. 11:29). I told this beautiful lady that I felt humble, so humble that I wanted to cry. She said, "Well, why don't you just cry then?" When she spoke, her voice exemplified her whole person, spirit and soul. The dream was like a movie, so detailed and so vivid. As I was going toward the freeway to hitch a ride back home, I started to cry. I felt so humble, I was still crying when I woke up!

To make a long story short, I didn't win "employee of the year," although I'd felt that there was no one close to me in the competition. When I looked back at that failure, it seemed that the dream was saying that I needed to be humbled before I was ready to receive honor. Although I had been a Christian for about eighteen years, the Lord was saying that I still wasn't ready to receive. It would be a long time before God gave me the victory in humility.

God's number *seven (7)* is completeness and totality in this particular area in my life it wouldn't come about easy. We must remember to humble ourselves under the mighty hand of God, that he may exalt us in due time (1 Peter 5:6). We must humble ourselves, and let God work.

That previous dream was connected to a dream I had just the other night. In this recent dream, I was at my *third (3)* job. As I went up the stairs, I heard one employee tell another that I (referring to me) had a nice home. God's words came to me: "My grace is sufficient for thee" (2 Cor. 12:9). To be exalted and highly favored is to have God's grace.

Sometime later, the company had a wine contest, but I didn't get involved. Not knowing what God thought of it, I stayed out of it. But when they offered money as an incentive to participate, I had second thoughts about it. The love of money is a root of all kinds of evil (1 Tim. 6:10). At that time, my church was going high-test. I was a deacon, and the head of the deacon board requested that we provide our own computers. I responded by saying that I had already put all my money into the church. Then I went to the Lord and I asked him about the wine contest. If he opened that door and allowed me to win the exact amount of money I needed, I would know that it was what he wanted me to do.

I don't remember the price of the computer, but I do remember that my participation in the contest was confirmed by God's numbers. After we received enough money for the computer which was a lot of money at that time my wife told me that we also needed a desk and a chair. I went back to work after *two (2)* days off (God's witness number). The manager told me and Jim Crossley, the waiter I'd teamed up with for about *twenty-five (25)* years, that we'd had another accumulation of funds. You won't believe the amount. It was the exact amount that we needed for the computer, desk and chair: $787.

Look at the amount we needed. *Seven (7)* is God's number (Gen. 2:2), the number of completeness. *Eight (8)* is His beginning number (Gen. 8:18), which involved eight (8) souls. Sometimes I call God's numbers His fingerprints. We have to be in the business of reading fingerprints, in this case, God's. He was saying, "I am Jehovah-Jireh," which meant "the Lord will provide" (Gen. 22:8–14). This was the times of God doing signs and wonders in my life, but it was not the last.

The second of the two sevens (7) meant *Elohim*, which was plural for God's covenant relationship, as well as an object of worship (Gen. 1:1; 2:3). From that point on, my work partner looked at my faith from a different perspective. The idea was to see God as a person and to perceive the things that He was beginning to do in my life.

Financing and Building the House

After paying off the land, I sought to find a construction loan. I went to two different banks, but neither one would give me the loan. They said I didn't have the experience to act as my own contractor. Even though I had the subcontractors lined up, I needed to get someone who was bonded to build the house. Although I had good credit and the land was paid off, there was too much money involved. I took my plans for the layout of the house, went home, and prayed about it.

After some time, I heard about a contractor right in my own neighborhood. He was even a Christian! We talked for a while, and I gave him a set of plans for the house. He said he would get back to me in a short period of time. It wasn't long before he came by my house and told me he would work with me, but there were some things we had to change. He said that we would have to split the subcontractors that he wanted to do the concrete, and that he would only charge me $3,500 as a contractor. Those numbers told me in retrospect that the Lord's fingerprints were saying that He has given me the victory and that His grace was sufficient for me (2 Cor. 12:9).

The contractor's name was Mr. Kline, and he always called me Mr. Anderson. Mr. Kline told me that he knew of a new bank that was giving out new loans and construction loans. It took some time to qualify, as we had to come up with more money and keep it in savings for six months to show that we were not using our last dollar. Eventually we were approved for the loan. We were very excited! God is good all the time!

The square footage of the house was 2,732. I had no idea what those numbers meant at the time. Now I know. *Two (2)* again means witnesses, *seven (7)* is God's number, and *three (3)* is God's victory number. There is a two (2) in front and in back, meaning that we would witness God's victory in the beginning and in the end. The height of the house, from the foundation to the peak, was *twenty-three*

(23) feet tall, which was also my number. From floor to ceiling was *twelve (12)* feet God's government number. I need not give Scripture for every fact, but I could not make this stuff up!

My wife Patsy had a vivid dream during the twelfth month of the year. She was on the Las Vegas strip with her fellow employees, when there was a great flood. She told them to follow her, because she and her husband were teaching about the end-times. The buildings were sinking, and my wife accidentally fell into the water, only to pop back up like a cork. Although the buildings were sinking, some of her fellow employees went back inside! This number twelve (12) tells me that when you are about the Father's business, nothing can harm or stop you. Praise God!

If you keep up with God's numbers, they will help guide your life. *Forty (40)* is a very important number. I was forty when I decided to buy the property on which to build. Some years later, I would meet the wife that God had for me. Pat was forty (40) when we met. We were separated by God's number *seven (7)* in age.

Moses' life was divided into *three forties*: 40, 80, and 120. For *forty (40)* days and nights, Moses was on the mountain with God to receive the commandments (Deut. 9:9). *Forty (40)* also can be a number of probation or a time of rest. Jesus was tempted in the wilderness by Satan for *forty (40)* days (Matt. 4:2). After *forty (40)* days, the spies returned from searching out the land of Canaan (Num. 13:25).

God is the same today as he was yesterday (Heb. 13:8). God is perfect and precise in what He does in your life, just as He is in his character and attributes. He says what He means and means what He says. Since I was sharing measurements of my own house, you can read Ezekiel 40 to look at the measurements of God's house. We serve an awesome God.

We started building our house, and everything was going fine. There were times when we had to wait on some of the subcontractors, simply because we were moving along so fast. There were also times when we would, for whatever reason, run out of money in certain areas, so I would go home and ask the Lord where the money would come from. He always opened my discernment as to where I could find the extra money.

My contractor said that he had never built a house in this manner. He told me in a gentle way that in other situations there was extra money, because the builders always had plenty of money available. He also said that this was a good experience for him. Now the subcontractors would be responsible for the estimates that had been given to the bank. The contractor would not be so liberal in his methods from that point on. We did have a carpenter who did not understand the layout of the house. It was a tri-level, which meant that the house was a single-story house with three levels in it. Since *three (3)* was the victory number of God, I believed we would have the victory.

The time came when we needed the trusses for the roof of the house, and we were sadly surprised to learn that the truss-building company had left town! We found out that we were not the only ones who had lost our money, as if that was any consolation. Some land developers lost as much as $60,000 or more. That slowed us to a standstill. I don't remember how long it took to get back on track, maybe because I don't want to remember. That mistake cost me $1,800. It was the first mistake that actually cost me money. The Lord was telling me that some things need to be learned. It's called experience. Not only did it cost me money, but it cost us time.

Later, we were all excited about the new trusses that we had ordered from Utah. The truck was supposed to come in on a Friday morning, but it broke down. We had to wait until Monday before they got the part for the truck, and then the trusses would get to us on Tuesday morning. That $1,800 loss made me take note of what God was telling me: that this would only be the beginning. Even after the house was built, we as homeowners must be on our guard. We were to be vigilant, for Satan would come as a roaring lion, seeking whom he may devour (John 10:10). Twenty-three (23) years later I would understand this.

From that time on, Satan was busy. My wife, to whom I had been married for *twelve (12)* years, came to me and said that she wanted a divorce. I was shocked! I finally talked some sense into her for a while. It seemed as if the Lord was saying that those twelve (12) years had been there for a reason. From that point on, I lost my blessings. The Lord was not pleased with my wife, so he put the blessings on hold. I believe the Lord was saying, "You can't be about my business until you get your house in order." I thank God for his grace and mercy.

The truck finally came roaring in on Tuesday morning as promised. The sky was so beautiful in the month of March: no clouds, no wind. As the crane was brought in, I started to notice the clouds and wind that came out of nowhere. All the workmen there also began to notice the weather. With the large crane, we completed the job, but when the wind and rain blew in, the men were very angry, and we all headed for our cars and trucks. The wind even blew some of the trusses off the house and broke them.

The head carpenter was very angry. Thank God we had builder's insurance. In retrospect, I realized that this happened on a Tuesday in March. That's the *third (3)* day of the week, and March is the *third (3)* month of the year, and both of these are God's number of victory. Jesus was victorious after three days in the heart of the earth, as was Jonah (Matt. 12:40). In Jonah's case the number three can also be the number of conclusion.

The Third Church

We were no longer going to the second church, the number of which (2) is God's number for "witness," but it was there that we started to discover our gifts. It was there Pastor Jefferson spoke out in prophecy, and cigarettes were taken away.

I was teaching men's Sunday school within six months. The pastor was so excited about the teaching that he attended every Sunday! We were there for about three and a half years, until we recognized that we had outgrown the church and some of their beliefs. We waited on the Lord.

This would be our third church, and *three (3)* is the "victory" number. When the Lord visited Abraham, He had two other angels with him (Gen. 18:1–14), which was a total of *three (3)*, the number of victory. The Lord said that He would visit them again at the same time a year later, meaning that Sarah would have a child. Is anything too hard for the Lord? Was it by accident that the number three was present in the biblical account? I say no. God is an organized God. All through the Bible, we see His numbers!

The pastor of our new church came from Los Angeles, California. A number of people came with him and his family. The church had its beginning on the *eleventh* day of the *seventh* (7) month. That day was a Sunday, which is the eighth (8) day, a new beginning (Rom. 6:4–5). On that same day, the pastor prophesied about me and another person. I was so shocked and excited, I didn't hear all his words! This would be the church in which my wife and I would see some of the amazing things I've already related. I once seen a person's leg grow right before my eyes!

I was one of *three (3)* new deacons that the pastor had chosen because of the growth of the church. In this case, it was the number of conclusion. On one particular Sunday, which is the number of new beginnings (Gen. 8:15–18), it was my turn to do the offering. I nervously stepped forward in faith, and at the very moment I began to speak, I could feel the energy and power of the Holy Spirit. He was carrying me and my words.

In retrospect, I realize that He was allowing me, through my faith, to see Him anoint my words using the number *three (3)*, which is the victory number. Although it never happened again, I always knew He was there. This took place in Joshua's situation, as he followed the Lord's instructions regarding the ark of the covenant, when the priests took a step of faith and were rewarded (Josh. 3:14–17). There was another time when I was to speak encouragement to the people, and I had my speech ready and prepared. As I spoke for a while, I could feel the Holy Spirit's anointing upon me. It got to the point where His presence was so great that I could only praise Him. Hallelujah!

We will see more of the number three (3) as we talk more about building my house and choosing my neighborhood. God's numbers are everywhere. As I come off the main street to my right is the very first house with the address 1077. After fifty or more years, new owners moved the mailbox from the side of the house to the front, which changed the address because the house was at the corner of two streets. Nevertheless, the old map showed the original address.

Ten (10) is God's number of completion or perfection in the Bible, depending on the context of the statement. His judgments sometimes come after ten (10) days, ten (10) months, or ten (10) years (1 Sam. 25:38), meaning that he will be perfect and complete in his justice and judgment (Ps. 89:14). (Also see Col. 2:10-4:12). We are complete and perfect in Christ, which is what I believe those numbers indicate. We also have completeness in the number seven (7), as well as in the number four (4).

The Lord once gave me a very vivid dream. I found myself and some members from my third church in a beautiful forest. The sky was very blue, and everything in the forest was beautiful! As I observed, I said to my brother in Christ, his wonderful wife, and my own lovely wife that my tree was taller than his. The Bible says that one man plants and one man waters, but God gives the increase (1 Cor. 3:6). He that waters and he that plants are one. The dream was saying that God was giving me the increase! This dream took place in August, which is the *eighth* month, in the year 2010. The Lord Jesus was saying in those numbers that he was going to begin to increase my blessings, more so spiritually, and that I would be complete in Him. Also, there were four (4) of us, God's complete number of creation (Eze. 1:10). Praise Him. At this time, September 10, 2010, God was really talking to me. (Notice the double *ten (10)* as well as the ninth (9) month, the fourfold of grace!

Hiding in Plain Sight

This next dream took place about two weeks after the previous dream.

I found myself being chased by evil men. I was informed in the dream that there was a reward out for me, a contract to cut my throat and kill me. In the dream, the Lord always gave me a way out, a way of escape. I slid off the top of a twenty- to thirty-foot building, and it was as if I was invincible. As the men chased after me, I heard a voice say, "He's trapped now. This is a dead end." I looked at all the locks on the big doors, and there was nowhere to go or to hide. I picked up a little telephone rack about the size of a small table lamp as a weapon, and even I had to laugh. In desperation, I lay down on a couch, thinking it was all over. But then my pursuers passed right by me! The Lord had hid me in plain sight! Praise God!

Once again, the Lord Jesus was using those double tens to say that I was perfect and complete in Him. If we stay in His perfect sacrifice, His perfect work, and His great atonement, we are blessed going in and going out, and everything we touch will prosper according to the will of the Father.

The first address in my neighborhood included *seventy-seven (77)*, two sevens the numbers of Elohim, which means God (Gen. 1:1; 2:3). We must worship Him. Praise is what you do, worship is who you are. When we go to church on Sunday we praise Him with our hearts, hands and lips, but when we leave we worship Him with our actions and words. Our lifestyle reveals who we worship.

When I left California in July 1973, I said that I would never look back. But I must look back on Jesus as I look ahead: I saw that with God's help, we were close to finishing a fairly good-size house. I looked back on the hard times in Mississippi off Highway 35, and I was deeply humbled. I remembered when I'd had whooping cough and nosebleeds that were so bad, I thought I would bleed to death. We'd had no car, so we were in the hands of God's mercy and grace. Those things that took place on Highway 35 that involved the number *five* (5) would bring victory with his marvelous grace. On Highway 35, I was able to get my first ticket out of that place to test the waters, so to speak.

When I was a child, Tadlock Stockyard Barn, was right off Highway 35, I was involved in a terrible car accident as a child. It was as if God was saying, this place owes you for the suffering you went through as a kid, I received no compensation for the mental agony. This was the place where I got my first real job. All those times that God sent me back and forth across the West, the Southwest, and the South, he was teaching me the things he wanted me to learn. I had no father, but I had God! He more than made up for what I needed. After all, he was a man on earth, the man Christ Jesus. He prepared me to build a house, but even more, He taught me to recognize the right choices, spiritually speaking. I had seen what the world could do to a person and to his health, and that it could bankrupt a person and leave him with nothing to show for it. There were many casino dealers who tried to win against the house, but didn't succeed.

A Word from the Lord

Many years later, my wife and I were getting things in order, and she purchased a new car. She was getting close to paying it off, and I was planning on getting another automobile. One day in 1998, I was driving down the street. It was my day-yes, the *twenty-third (23)*. When I approached the traffic light, the Lord spoke very strong to my spirit and said, "Don't get another car. You have already put enough money into this one. Pay off the mortgage on house, and then you can do other things independently."

I went home and told my wife what the Lord had told me. From that point on, we concentrated on exactly that. We started by making extra payments, sending in additional money on the house note. We got into a bi-weekly program. God's victory number *three (3)* was also the number that God gave me on the *twenty-third (23)* day (my number) of March (the *third (3)* month and God's victory number). Getting to that point with my car was not easy, the car being twenty years old, but the Lord was saying to trust him.

One day as I was talking to the Lord, I told Him that I had a problem with the smell of gas when the car was running. I had taken the car to the shop, but Doug my mechanic couldn't find the leak. I would stop the car, leave it running, and then get out to look. I could see the drops of gas leaking under the car, but when I stopped the car, it stopped leaking—no more smell, no more leak. This was very nerve-racking. One time I was driving down the freeway when a guy threw out a cigarette. I almost had a heart attack! However, God had spoken to me, and I still had a lot of faith in Him.

This went on for a while. The Devil said things like, "Do you have your life insurance paid up? One night when you get off work, your car will have blown up from a cigarette or some other form of fire." I had to stay firm in my faith, telling myself that I was in Christ and that I would not focus on fear.

One day as I was coming home, the Lord gave me the victory. When I stopped the car in the garage and got out, the leak was still dripping, and I could see where it was coming from. I took a small piece of something and forced it up in there. Later Doug fixed it. This was the *tenth (10)* day of the *seventh (7)* month of 2008. God's number seven was my total completeness in Jesus. In the Bible, *ten (10)* is God's number of completeness (Matt. 25:28). The *eight (8)* in 2008 is saying the number of beginning (Gen. 8:18). I knew I would begin to see God's blessings, signs, and wonders.

Satan didn't lie down and give up. He never does. But the Lord would give me the victory in all *three (3)* areas in my life.

A Warning to Pray on Interstate 15

One evening a few years earlier, I was going to work in the Cadillac Seville. I was going quite fast on the freeway, when I had a very strong urge to pray for the car—that it would hold together, that nothing would happen to it. I made it to work in one piece, got out of the car, and looked around—and saw nothing! I went to work, trying not to think of what had happened.

After work, I got in the car, drove to the store right next to the strip, went into the store, came out, and got back in the car. I tried to turn onto the strip to get to the freeway, but the car kept going straight ahead as if I wasn't steering it! I backed up, and the same thing happened again. I had no steering! I finally managed to get the car parked. I sat there for a while, realizing the danger that would have happened if I had gotten onto the freeway.

I also thought about my sudden urge to pray. I hadn't imagined it. The Lord had directed me to pray, and the angels had held the car together long enough for me to get to a safe place before they released it! Praise God! Those are exciting words. Fear took over my thoughts as I thought about what could have happened on that freeway driving seventy miles per hour and suddenly losing control of my steering. Here is the love of God. Why didn't He allow the incident to happen in the parking lot at work, as opposed to it happening at the store? Because God is always concern with the little things as well. He knew I needed something at the store, so He allowed it after I came out of the store. Thank you Jesus!

That is what the Lord does in our lives all the time. Most of the time we are not aware of what is happening in, and around our lives. It's called *divine providence.* The prayers of a righteous man avail much (James 5:16). The Lord's grace was sufficient for me (2 Cor. 12:9). The number of Interstate 15 includes the number *one (1),* which could indicate a personality, an individual, or a person. Jesus said, "The Father and I are one (1)" (John 10:30). *Eloah* means "deity, God, the divine one (1)" (Deut. 32:15, 17; 2 Chron. 32:15; Neh. 9:17).

The other number of Interstate 15 is *five (5)*, which is the number of grace. Of all the names of God, this one is the greatest and has to do with Jesus. Given in the incarnation, it means "Savior" (Matt. 1:21). John said that Jesus brought grace and truth (John 1:17). Interstate 15 was the freeway I had come in from California many years earlier. Except for a terrible chemical spill that held up traffic for over an hour, making me late for work, I have gone almost forty (40) years without an accident on Interstate 15. I thank God for this. That chemical spill took place about a mile from work, and the Lord gave me a warning. From that point on, I always prayed on the way to work.

I can't say that I have been entirely accident-free, for I have had some very close calls with my car. I have had two major accidents. The first one was a four- or five-car accident. A guy ran a stoplight, causing the event. I was hit on the driver's side of my car. The whole thing seemed to happen in slow motion. I was trapped between two cars. It was as if those two cars held me in place while the other car rammed into me with nowhere to go. The place where the car was struck made the difference in the car not being totaled out. It was the defense pole, if I can use that term, which protected the A-frame from being hit. Praise God!

The other major accident took place, ironically, in front of a car dealership. As I was waiting at a light, I was struck from behind. The other driver never saw me. There were smaller accidents as well. The Lord gave me the right car for the duration, for it is still running after *thirty-five (35)* years!

Blessings of the Lord

God's plan for my life involved my being married, and she had to be a Christian. We had to have some of the same spiritual gifts and the same calling. One night when I came home from work, the Lord showed me exactly that.

I had just come in the door, and I noticed that my wife had left me a note on the table. It said, "Honey, I need the old calendar so I can get some of the old dates from it. I could not find it. Love, Pat." I had thrown the calendar into the trash, so I went out to the garage to search for it, leaving the door partway open. Suddenly I noticed Pat standing in the doorway, rubbing her eyes, which shocked me. Usually she was fast asleep, and she only knew I was home when I came into the bedroom. At that time we did not have a security alarm. I asked her," why was she up?" she had been told that there was a door open! I was shocked and speechless. There had been other similar revelations.

At this time, the Lord was blessing me at the church. On Tuesday, the *third (3)* day of the week, the pastor called me to confirm my being on the deacon board. This was also the *seventeenth (17)* day of the month, which is God's number. Around that same time, I was also blessed on the job after working there for *twenty-eight* years.

Our home was also blessed by the Lord. We were fighting for a security wall around our neighborhood, but *two* obstacles stood in the way: city hall and some neighbors who were stuck in their ways. However, we would witness God's favor, an attribute of grace. We gave it to God and we did our part. Two of my Christian brothers and I had a plan to get up early one morning and claim the victory—that the wall was ours. Just as Nehemiah had favor with the king and God gave Israel victory (Neh. 2:4–6), we too had victory! God gave the *three (3)* of us the victory that morning for the wall. There was a spiritual wall that had to be defeated as well. (Matthew 16:18) says that the gates of hell shall not prevail against us. We may not think about numbers being in our lives, but God is a God of order (1 Cor. 14:40; 14:33). He tells us to set our house in order (2 Kings 20:1).

There are two numbers I want to focus on concerning the church. We had a board at church that consisted of *seven (7)* people. I occupied the (7) seat. In retrospect, I know that I was in that chair for a reason. This didn't become obvious until the death of the pastor. We will discuss that more in detail later. This was my *third (3)* church, where I would get God's victory. However, the deacon position was only meant for me to learn what God had for me before moving forward and being ordained as an elder.

Before I was divorced from my first wife, the Lord spoke to me in a very real way. At that time I had not joined any church, but I was watching and getting my spiritual food on TV. Also, I was very dedicated to reading the Bible and other Christian material. I remember receiving the baptism of the Holy Spirit according to Acts 1:8. I began to notice God more intimately and to have a stronger relationship with him. My wife and I had only been in our house for about a year and a half when everything started to unravel.

Seven Words

Once again, my wife started to rebel, and the children started to act up. One morning in May, the *fifth (5)* month, the month of grace, I woke up from a nightmare, something I hadn't experienced in a while, for the Lord had given me sweet sleep (Prov. 3:24). As I lay in bed, I asked the Lord why all these things were beginning to happen to me once again. I wasn't expecting an answer at least, not in the way he was going to speak to me.

Someone might ask how I knew it was God's voice. Could it have been some other type of spirit? The Lord said that His sheep knows His voice (John 10:4). Also, His number *seven (7)* was in His answer. He spoke *seven (7)* words to me, and I quote: "He is trying to destroy your will!" I was shocked, excited, and mildly afraid. I lay there for a while and considered what had just taken place, examining the words, thinking about their meaning. The

Lord Jesus—in this case, the Holy Spirit—was saying that the Enemy was coming at me.

As I read the book of Job, I understood that a person doesn't have to be sinning for the Devil to attack him. The Lord allows it for His purpose and plan in our lives. He tells us to be sober and vigilant against our adversary the Devil (1 Peter 5:8). Two of the nine (9) gifts of the Spirit were in operation: a word of knowledge was piggybacking the spirit of discernment. The gift of discernment enables a person to hear or see into the spirit world, whether it involves man, demons, fallen angels, or God's Spirit himself. A word of knowledge is exactly that: a word from God.

At that point, I waited for more, but it never came. Those words would speak volumes to my spirit, for the hell was just beginning. A few years later, the Lord would give me a dream acknowledging those facts. Highway 35 was starting all over again, but this time I was closer to Jesus. I knew him better, and I was much more mature in Christ, to put it mildly. After a divorce, and many heartaches, my son Michael was planning to go into the army, and I received a vivid dream from the Lord.

I dreamed that, as I was coming home from work, I saw a fire in the back bedroom of the house. I ran into the house, expecting to see the whole house on fire, but it was only Michael's bedroom, and I found that the fire had burned itself out. The fire had not touched his bed, and he was still asleep. The interpretation was this: he would go through the fire, but not a hair on his head would be burned.

There are many people in prison today who are innocent. When Michael was facing eighty to ninety years in prison, he was out in under seven. Once again, this was God's number *seven (7)* his completeness and totality. During the time Michael was in prison, he was protected. Praise God!

The Lord has allowed many things to happen in my life for his glory and to strengthen me, that I might have a testimony for others. Through trials come trust, faith, perfect patience, and humility so that God can use us. Faith is tested when it is great, and it is tested to make it great. God can use us on a wider scale when we are chastened, for it proves that he loves us (Heb. 12:6). It is for our benefit.

In my current location, I make a right-hand turn off the main street onto Ophir, which is a street in the Bible (2 Chron. 8:18; Job 22:24; 1 Kings 10:11). It is a place where there is gold. Gold symbolizes God's glory, protection, and power. That, by itself, is a great start! This street joins together with Sharon Road, which is also in the Bible. Sharon is the broad, rich tract of land that stretches southward from the foot of Mount Carmel and melts into the Shefelan, a plain noted for its flowers: hence, roses of Sharon and forest. Lebanon, Sharon, Carmel, and Bashan are the four (4) most beautiful regions of the Holy

Land (Isa. 33:9; Acts 9:35). Four (4) being the complete number of creation.

The Numbers and Life on Sharon Road

As I looked at the numbers on Sharon Road, the first thing I saw were the Devil's numbers. I never gave the Holy Spirit the space or chance for His divine revelation of the meaning. You see, I had been trained by superstition, Hollywood, and Friday the thirteenth (13). I had already prejudged the number. It has been revealed to me, that the number thirteen (13) is a hidden number of victory in the bible, if I may use the word. Joseph was in slavery for a period of thirteen (13) years (Gen. 37:2; 41:46) before ruling as prime minister of Egypt. Joshua and the children of Israel, marched around the city of Jericho thirteen (13) times (Josh. 6:3-4) and there were thirteen apostles with Matthias (Acts 1:26). Thirteen (13) tribes of Israel with the tribe of Levite (Num. 26:5-57). Thirteen (13) years from covenant to circumcision (Gen. 16:16-17:1; 24-25).

One of the most important chapters in the Bible is in 1 Corinthians 13, the "love chapter". There are other ways to look at the number thirteen (13)," my address was 1301 Sharon. First, we have the number *one (1)*, and then we have the number *three (3)*. God is *one (1)*, for Jesus said that He and the Father are one. But *one (1)* is plural when it comes to God. The word *Elohim* means God. The number *three (3)* can also mean three individual Gods as well. Then we have *one (1)*. *One (1)* means that we are back where we were with *one (1)*, which means that God is *one (1)*.

Another way to look at the numbers of the address is this: God has given, is giving, and will give me the victory on Sharon Road. A lot of things have happened to me and my beautiful wife at 1301, but there is one experience that really stays in our souls and spirits. My wife and I had gone down south for our fourth or fifth wedding anniversary. The doctor had told me that I could have some wine if I wanted it, and it was tempting to me at that time. I was only an usher at the church, so I reasoned with myself that perhaps it was all right, as long as I was having it with dinner.

We decided to get a bottle of champagne and celebrate. We got to the point where we had a coffee cup with wine in it while we drove. As we were on Interstate 20 going back to the airport, we noticed a highway patrol car coming up beside us and then dropping back. We also noticed that there were two other patrol cars on the dividers as we continued down the road. Not only were the other two cars following us, but now there was a helicopter above us.

I told Pat that I thought they were following us. We started to move into plan B. We slid the bottle of champagne under the seat of the car, finished the remainder of the champagne in the cups, took a couple of mints, and started to pray that if the Lord would get us out of this, we would never drink in the car again! We thought that we were part of a movie scene, as they swooped in on us from every side. The lights and everything were on, and we finally got the hint and pulled over.

A big, black sheriff, who looked like John Wayne, came to the car with another officer. I got out of the car, hoping to draw fire away from the car, and met them halfway. The sheriff came to me, and the other officer went to my wife's side of the car. The sheriff questioned me about where we were going and where we were from. After answering all his questions, he looked at my driver's license. Apparently the other officer had already asked to see the registration of our rented vehicle. It appeared that the rental company had taken our tags off another car, and they did not match the one we were driving!

After they had checked the information out, we were okay to leave. We thanked God all the way to the airport, and we never had another cup of anything in the car again. By God's grace and mercy, we learned a lot from that experience. Regarding Interstate 20, *two (2)* is the "witness" number (John 8:17–18). We have a daughter who lives on Interstate 20, which also goes through my wife's hometown, all the way to my hometown, and finally to Alabama the hometown of our pastor. My Cadillac Seville was shipped from Abilene, TX off 20. But nothing witnessed to us like that last experience.

We were admonished by the number *thirteen (13)*. Romans 13:1–4 says:

> Let every soul be subject unto the higher powers. For there is no power but of God: the powers that be are ordained of God. Whosoever therefore resisteth the power, resisteth the ordinance of God: and they that resist shall receive to themselves damnation. For rulers are not a terror to good works, but to the evil. Wilt thou then not be afraid of the power? Do that which is good, and thou shalt have praise of the same: for he is the minister of God to thee for good. But if thou do that which is evil, be afraid; for he beareth not the sword in vain: for he is the minister of God, a revenger to execute wrath upon him that doeth evil.

Chapter 13 is a very important chapter. God was telling us that He sees and knows everything. Just when we thought we were so smart that no one would be the wiser, we were completely wrong. This is how the Lord leads people and lawbreakers to law enforcement. We hear all the time that people have been caught because a taillight was out. We also have a grandson whom I have already mention, He was born on the (13th) day. Also a granddaughter –Mikayla who was born the year of (2000), which makes her (13) this year.

If I may, I will bore you with the number *thirteen (13)* once more. At age *sixty-four (64)*, we have *thirteen (13)* grandkids, and at age *fifty-seven (57)*, I was a great grandfather. Notice that the number *fifty-seven (57)* refers to God's grace and completeness. Also, God's number *seven (7)* is the span of (7) years between fifty-seven and sixty-four.

Let us talk about the neighbors' numbers. The neighbor's address next door is 1231, which was amazing! *Twelve (12)* refers to God's government (Rev. 21:12, 14). Also, my number *twenty-three (23)* is in there, and the last number is again *one (1)*. Across the street, directly in front of my house, is the number 1250. Every time I look across the street at that number, I am reminded of God's government and grace. It is also the number and year of Jubilee (Lev. 25: 10-11).

As I think back on that number of grace, I am reminded of my youngest daughter, Jami. When she was *five (5)*, her mother and I were separated, waiting to finalize our divorce. She wanted to spend the night with me. I realized that she had some form of a nightmare when she woke up screaming. I asked her if she had a bad dream. She said, "Yeah, Daddy!" She said that there was something hideous in the bathroom in the folded towels. I asked her if she would like to accept Jesus as her Lord and Savior. She was excited and said, "Yes, Daddy! Yes, Daddy!" I told her to repeat a prayer of salvation after me. Later, she told me that she never had that kind of dream again. I told her that Jesus had taken away the bad dreams.

Was that a coincidence? There are no coincidences with God. The number of her age was the number of grace, and God is a great planner. Losing my daughter was the most hurtful part of the divorce. When her mother moved back south, I prayed to the Lord and told Him the kind of wife that I wanted, since He had sent the other one packing and had told me not to go chasing after her. God is so good. A few years later after my x wife and daughter had moved back south, doing the Christmas season there was a very popular toy on the market at that time. My daughter wanted one, but they were short in supply. There wasn't any in the state she was in, or any other place at the time. Time was running out on finding one. I went to this one store looking for one but they were out as well. I remember praying to the Lord about someone returning one back to the store. As I was leaving the store, the store manager spoke on the intercom for me to return to the store manager. Someone had returned one to the store! We also had to get the toy to my daughter about three or four days before Christmas, which was almost impossible from Vegas to the south. We just happen to have my wife's sister Carol in town! She only lived about forty five miles away from them! God cares about the little things in our lives as well. This was the twelfth (12) month. When we are about His government, He's about our business. I believed also, that wife was in the making.

Coming home after work was the hardest part. I was used to someone being at home when I got home from work. It wasn't long before I knew I had to make a change, because I'd never realized how large the house was until I came home to its dark emptiness. I guess you could say that I was going to help God find that wife. I must confess that I had an affair. It did not work out, and I repented to God. Actually, I had two girlfriends before I repented to the Lord for making shamble out of everything. I also realized that perhaps the Lord was preparing my wife for me as well, for no one is perfect.

When I met the third (3) woman, I knew she would not be my next girlfriend but the wife that I had patiently waited for! I had told the Lord that I wanted someone who knew about life, someone to whom I could tell anything and be trusted. There was a place called the Moulin Rouge, where Sammy Davis Jr. and Sinatra had come years earlier. I asked myself, why was I there, it was not a place for a Christian. I reasoned that I was a Christian, so there must be some Christian woman there as well.

Satan loves divorces. He breaks up the home so that there is no father in the house and sometimes no mother. In retrospect, I saw that it was one of the best things that could have happened in my life. I would be able to appreciate a good and strong Christian wife when I got one, and we would grow in the Lord together. The Moulin Rouge was built in 1955, which was the same year that my wife was born. Also, there are double fives (5) on both of my vehicles' license plates. The number *fifty-five* (two fives) means double grace. The place was built on a street called Bonanza, which was the name of the area I lived in: Bonanza Village. Bonanza Street went east and west, and the last address to the east was 2300, and the last address to the west was also 2300! What was it about the number twenty-three (23)? Why did this number pop up so often in my life?

We have a daughter who desired to have a child. She finally got pregnant and was able to carry the baby for *thirty-seven (37)* weeks. She started out in room number *seven (7)*. The baby girl was born on—you guessed it— the *twenty-third (23)*. They named her LaMya. Let us examine the numbers. *Two (2)* is the number of witness (Rev. 11:3); *three (3)* is the number of victory (Gen. 18:1–2; Judg. 7:6–7). We can also put the two numbers together, and we have the number of grace. Sometimes the numbers can piggyback to make one number. In Matthew 14:17, we have *five* loaves and *two* fish, which add up to the number *seven (7)*. I believe these numbers are in everyone's life if they look for them.

There are times when I will have a dream, wake up, and look at the digital clock—and the numbers are in agreement with my dreams. One may ask, what is the purpose of the numbers? You know, when I was in the world, I was into horoscopes, and I threw out everything but the personality. After observing and studying individuals born in each month, I saw that people born in the same month had a lot in common with each other. Once God created the chicken, the eggs were automatic. What I am saying is this: God's numbers comes with circumstances and events. Look for his fingerprints. I believe that a person takes part of his personality from the month in which he was born, from his family genes, and from his culture and the rest is individuality.

I have come to the point now, that when I see God's numbers whether they are past or present, they give me an idea of what He's doing. For instance, I received a word from the Lord, "the third (3)" and "eyewitness." It was amazing that on the *third* (3) day of that month, we received the victory on something that we had been dealing with for *three* (3) years. It's as if everything was lined up to coincide with the numbers. "Eyewitness" meant that the two (2) of us would witness it. The Lord had prophesied this would happen!

There was a time when my ex-wife and I got into a disagreement, the police came to our house, and someone had to go to jail. My patience had run out. But the Lord was with me. I had been in jail for *two* days without anyone knowing I was there, when my pity party was finally over. I didn't have any money with me, so the Lord told me to go down to the area where the bail bond numbers were and pick the first name and number on the paper. I called the number, and a lady answered the phone. I told her my situation and that I had no money with me. She knew the contractor who had built my house, and I told her that once I got out, I would get the money and pay her. Bright and early that morning, I was bailed out! She was a very sweet lady, and God gave me favor with her. Her business was at Bonanza and Main. The building address was 500 Bonanza, *five (5)* being the number of grace. What a blessed street Bonanza was for me!

The sweet wife that the Lord gave me was exactly what I had prayed for. The Lord had even given me her birth month. Over time, I got familiar with her personality. The women I knew who had been born in that month were always ones who had been hurt and disappointed, and they were always friends with sweet personalities. So I had told the Lord that this was the kind of wife for me.

I asked to visit my future wife for the first time when I noticed her address! It was 1237! I could not believe it. *Twelve (12)* was God's government, *twenty-three (23)* was my number, and God's number *seven* was on the end. God's fingerprints were all over her, including Bonanza Street and her house number. God is good all the time, and all the time God is good! The Lord was blessing my wife and me in all three (3) areas of our lives: the *third (3)* church, the job, and 1301 Sharon Road. *Three (3)* was the victory number. I was attending my *third (3)* church and was on my *third (3)* job, which would be my retirement job.

When I'd first come to town, I had worked at the Dunes Hotel for one year. I did the fire at the MGM at that time and went to work at the Aladdin for six weeks, which made that my second job. During my thirty-eight years on the strip in Vegas, those were the only *three (3)* jobs I had. So God had given me victory through the number *three (3)* once again.

He also gave me victory in the (3) *third* house, which would be my dream home, the house that I would build without experience. People were moving out of that area to more popular areas, and the housing market was starting to boom. My area was an older area that had large lots, and I got my property very cheap! However, I still had to have faith in the Lord. I was getting ready to spend more money on the house than anyone had spent in that area for a long time. But I stayed there in faith, as people continued to move out. God had given me the vision, so I stayed the course.

Since that time, we have had nine (9) new houses and twenty-seven (27) remodeled homes. The numbers was saying, we was witnessing Him and His fourfold grace. God never led me wrong. Meanwhile, in the church, God was starting to speak to me again, mostly in dreams. The pastor decided to have a "men only" retreat in Palm Desert. There would be no wives, only men for *five* (5) days, which was the number of grace. My wife and I had not been apart in the *eight* (8) years we had been married, from 1995 to 2003. The number *eight* (8) is the number of new beginning, and this explains the eight (8) years. You never think about the time, until you start to write about it. A lot of the numbers had been recorded, as the Lord had given me a burden to write them down. This shows that these numbers are precise in my life. I talked to the Lord about the matter of leaving my wife to go on this retreat, because the pastor had said that all leadership had to go!

CHAPTER 3

A Word from the Lord

Pastor Jackson was his name. He said that we needed to get away from all the distractions so that we could hear a word from the Lord. My mother lived in Banning, California, so I told my pastor that I wanted to stay with my mother while I was there. He agreed that I should spend time with my mother after the meetings and fellowship were over in the afternoon. I went screaming and kicking, but once I knew I was going, I asked the Lord to speak to me and make himself known to me. I needed to look forward to the spiritual benefits instead of dreading my wife not being there.

We left on May 22, and the weather was nice in California. The next day, I drove to the retreat from my mother's house, which was only about half an hour away. Besides the men from my church, there were men from other churches that were affiliated with our church. There was a lot of activity going on in every area of the hotel. Two hundred men were in a large room, where we prayed and interceded. When it was over, we met with our pastor and group, and then we were told to go and have breakfast.

As we were gathering around, one of the pastor's men from another group came by and said that the Lord had told him to ask me where I was in the ministry. At that time I was a deacon, and I told him so. He said, "The Lord said, 'I put you there." I was shocked and amazed. The men who were standing by were shocked as well. He continued by saying, "You know, I don't know anything about this. Does it minister to you? Were you expecting something from the Lord?" I said yes. The whole group of men around us continued to talk about it.

I was on a spiritual high for about twenty-four hours. The numbers were right on time: it was May, the *fifth (5)* month, which was God's number of grace. The day was the *twenty-third (23)*, which was no surprise. This was exactly eleven years ago to the day that I was baptized and having an experience that I would not soon forget. The Spirit of God was on me that day in a powerful way. I went to my mother's house and told her about it, and she was very excited. As the power of the Holy Spirit was on me, I asked her if she would like to be baptized and filled with the Holy Spirit. She was excited and said yes!

I laid hands on her and prayed with her, and she was filled with the Holy Spirit. That is a different function from being born of the spirit. She revealed to me that if she had not been sitting down at the time, she would possibly have fallen down! This was a gift from the Lord (Luke 11:11–13; Acts 1:8–2:4), and she was never the same. After a time, she eventually stopped smoking, and she gave up the one can of beer as well. That was something she had wanted to do. She had not been pressured to do it.

I came back to Vegas refreshed, with a different perspective. The Lord had come to me in a dream and said, "Where you are going, there will be no wine!" He came to me in the form of someone with great wisdom and discernment, someone with a white beard. The dream was more of a spiritual sense, for He spoke to my spirit. By reading the pastoral epistle I understood that I had been called to the ministry.

At that time, judging by the Scriptures, I could have a couple of glasses of wine per week, being a deacon. But when I became an elder, I continued to have those two glasses of wine per week. The Lord didn't bring it up at that time.

On Sunday morning, I would meet up with other people to intercede for the church and others. One Saturday night I got off work about three hours early. My wife was serving dinner, and I said I was going to have a glass of wine with dinner. I reasoned that it would be okay. Never mind that it was less than fourteen hours before I would have to intercede for the church. When I reached for the bottle of wine, the Holy Spirit came to me with a strong force. From that day until now, I have never had the Holy Spirit come to me like that. There was no word, but you knew he was saying no! To whom much is given, much is required (Lk.12:48).

For about nineteen months or so, the Lord said nothing more regarding the wine. Then, one New Year's Eve, I had a nightmare. It was very scary! The next weekend after having wine, I once again experienced a nightmare. I told my wife about it and said I believed it was the wine. I also told her the contents of the dream. I told her I'd dreamed that some hideous creature was after me. As I was closing the door on its horrifying hand, I left a crack in the door. I realized that the Lord was telling me that I was now an elder, and that he couldn't protect me, for I was leaving a door open for the Enemy. I told my wife I was going to stop drinking wine, because it was not enjoyable to the flesh any longer. I had a long talk with the Lord and told him I would not have any more wine. I asked Him to bless me spiritually and to replace the wine with His blessings.

I believe the Lord has given me an understanding about wine. Deuteronomy 14:26 says, "And you shall bestow that money for whatsoever your soul lusts after [desires], for oxen, or for sheep, for wine or strong drink, or whatsoever your soul desires: and you shall eat there before the Lord your God, and you shall rejoice, you and your household". Numbers 6:2–4, 20 says "That a person who takes a Nazirite vow must not drink wine or anything that has to do with the grapevine. But when the ceremony is over, Nazirites may drink wine again". Proverbs 23:20–21 speaks against gluttony and drunkenness, which means that God has always been against those two things.

Let us look at (Rom. 14:21). Paul said, "It is good neither to eat flesh, nor to drink wine, nor anything whereby thy brother stumbleth, or is offended, or is made weak." Paul also told Timothy to have a little wine as medicine for his stomach. Romans 14:17 says, "For the kingdom of God is not meat and drink; but righteousness, and peace, and joy in the Holy Spirit." There are other Scriptures, but this one makes the point and establishes His Word. I believe the Lord is saying that, because people didn't have the Holy Spirit in the Old Testament, he allowed them to have wine or strong drink, providing they didn't get drunk (Prov. 23:20–21).

Kraipale comes from the Greek word *kra*, or "head," and means to agitate a headache, a shooting pain in the head arising from intemperance in drinking wine and strong liquor. It is translated in Luke 21:34 as *surfeiting*, the sense of disgust and loathing from being full of wine. Jesus was using this very word when he said, "Take heed to yourselves, lest at any time your hearts be overcharged with surfeiting, and drunkenness, and the cares of this life, and so that day comes upon you unawares."

Jesus was speaking of the second coming. Ecclesiastes 9:7 says, "Go eat your bread with joy, and drink your wine with a merry heart; for God has already accepted your works." People didn't have the joy of the Holy Spirit or His divine revelations then as we do now. He now comes into our hearts and lives and dwells there. Thank Jesus, our Lord, for His cross that makes it possible! That makes it clearer than ever that we now have the Holy Spirit, the Comforter. We have the wine of the Holy Spirit.

The sooner we realize that the Holy Spirit is all we need, the better off we are. Praise God. Some of us have to grow to that point. The pastor said that he needed someone to teach Bible study on Thursday at *ten (10)* o'clock. Thursday is the *fifth (5)* day of the week, which is the day of grace or the number of grace (Gen. 15:9).

A Sign from the Book of Revelation

The pastor called and asked me if I would teach Bible study on Thursday. I told him yes, if he would permit me to teach what I wanted. At that time, he was being treated for cancer and needed time to rest. He was very excited for me. I went to the Lord and asked Him if it was okay, if He would give me a sign to let me know that it was okay to teach from the book of Revelation.

One night as I was lying in bed, I saw something on the ceiling of my bedroom. I didn't know what was going on. It was very scary and looked like something on an iodine bottle, white as snow. Then, all at once, like when Peter saw his vision, the thing folded itself up and went back up through the ceiling of the house! As I lay in the bed, I asked myself, what I had just seen. Confused and uncomfortable, it came to me that I had asked the Lord for a sign to confirm my teaching a particular Scripture for Bible study. He was showing me that when I stopped the wine, he would bless me more and reveal more to me. Surely, as I came closer to Him, he would come closer to me. I was very pleased and grateful to the Lord, for surely I had just received a vision from the Lord!

The Lord really blessed the Bible study. He gave me great revelation and understanding. It was as if Phillip was asking the question, "Do you understand what you are reading?" The Spirit of God was always there. God is no respecter of persons (2 Chron. 19:7). He will do the same for you, for everyone has a calling, and you must answer that call. The Bible says that many are called, but few are chosen. Actually, all are called, but few answer the call (John 3:16, Rev. 22:17).

Hezekiah in a Book

The Lord showed me one night in May, which was the grace month, that His grace was sufficient for me, for His strength was made perfect in weakness (2 Cor. 12:9). Hezekiah was shown to me in a book, and I got up in order to understand and not lose the message.

Half-asleep, I realized that Hezekiah was not a book, but a true story in a book: the Bible. After reading the story, which I already knew, I expected to see something that I hadn't realized before, and I saw what the Lord was telling me. The Lord was saying that I had been healed, just like Hezekiah!

What a revelation! I was so excited and relieved. For years the Enemy had been telling me a lie, telling me that I was not healed, that I was going to die young like my uncles from liver disease. The Lord gave me the victory. That revelation would be a plus in the events to come.

What is it about May? So many things have happened in that month. My wife and I lost a son in the month of May, on the same day as my brother, Willie's birthday. When everyone was grieving, the Lord told my wife not to worry, for Joseph was now with Him. He is an on-time God. Yes, He is!

The Experience of a UFO

In the month of May as I sat on the back patio, I noticed a helicopter hanging over the trees and making no sound. That got my attention. It was perhaps half a mile from the house. We lived in the city limits, about half a mile from downtown. There was a small airport in north town not far from where this helicopter was.

I asked my wife to come and see the helicopter that wasn't making any sound. As she came outside to see it, it began to move. All at once, it started to change shape as it moved. It floated across the sky in slow motion, like a piece of trash in the wind. I remember being disappointed and telling Pat that it was only a piece of trash. Pat responded by saying that trash didn't go across the sky in a straight line. I already knew that, but I needed to hear her say it. Years earlier, when I had been delving into horoscopes, UFOs had been part of my fascination. When my spirit was not in play, I became fascinated by other means. But now I knew the Lord in a higher and more experienced way. I no longer had any interest in UFOs—until now.

As this thing went over the neighbors' houses, I couldn't see it anymore, and I didn't want to know if it had disappeared or not. I felt some type of fear. My wife had never cared for UFOs, nor was she interested in them. I knew there was some kind of fear within her as well. To this day, I don't know why the Lord allowed my wife and me to see this experience. It was as if God was saying to me, "So, you really want to know whether or not UFOs exist?" Well, from that point on, I did not doubt that we had seen something that we could not explain. God's grace plays many and all parts.

While we are on the subject of weird things, I will share something that happened on May 27, 2012, in the month that is the number of God's grace. Pat and I witnessed

God's totality and completeness in his government. Many people have seen the documentary called *The Body*, which was aired on two different channels. Some people were trying to cover it up, just the way they tried to cover Jesus up by wrapping him in a nice little package and keeping Him in the grave. Why is it that government and religion try to make our decisions for us?

Thank God for the National Day of Prayer on the *fifth* (5) day of May (the *fifth* (5) month). How ironic that the numbers indicate double grace in the dispensation of grace. Thank God for Jesus, who brought grace and truth to this great country centuries ago. *Fifty (50)* years ago in the month of May (1961), the Freedom Riders took a bus from Fisk University. In May 1945, Germany surrendered on the first day of May. President Obama acknowledged that Osama Bin Laden was dead. By God's wonderful grace, I met my wife in May.

The list goes on, as I have already revealed other things that happened in May. July, the *seventh* (7) month, is God's number (Lev. 23:8). There are seven (7) annual feast days (Rev. 5:12) and God's sevenfold blessing.

The year was 2006, and I was in and out of consciousness the morning that the Lord spoke these words to me: "Fire is hard to get started."

Fire Is Hard to Get Started

At that time, I thought the Lord was talking about the church, which I will discuss later. There were many things that the Lord was telling me. One of those things was about prophecy. Unless a specific date was given, prophecies germinate over a period of time (Ezek. 28:8). God's word and a dream came to me in the year 2010, the number of completeness in the Bible (Matt. 25:28).

I perceived three *sevens (7)* and the Lord saying, "We will be with you tomorrow!" I believe the Lord was talking about (2012). Also, the Lord started to speak to me in 1991. From 1991 to 2012 is *twenty-one* (21) years): hence, the three (3) sevens. Also, 2012 is God's number of government.

The amazing thing is that the words in the dream referred to God as *we*. God is one, but each person of the Godhead has His own function. For instance, the Holy Spirit is the only God here on earth now, and He dwells within us. The Lord Jesus is the High Priest, the Mediator between God and man. He makes it possible for God's children to speak with the Father and have a relationship with Him. Everything is done according to the will of the Father.

God's Victory Number the Hard Way

My wife and I were discussing our desire for another set of French doors to the patio. The ones we had were getting a little old, and the weather-stripping was no longer serving its purpose. One night I received a word from the Lord. He said that my wife and I would each receive $1,500. I remember asking Him, "Are you sure it isn't $15,000?" I got no reply.

My wife and I wondered how this would come about, we had no idea. As time passed, we had a burglary in our home. You won't believe this. The thief came in through the patio French doors! He only took two of my watches and an old cell phone. He did some damage to the walls and poured soda on one of the sofas. I guess he was upset because he couldn't find anything of value. I believe the Lord gave the thief a spirit of fear, for I was only gone from the house for about forty minutes. At that time, we had no alarm, for we'd never had a break-in. You could say that the Lord was collecting off our home insurance after seventeen years (17).

We had no fear, for we knew that this was from the Lord. It was another three or four years before we finally got an alarm. The kids were worried for us, for we had already planned a vacation to Albuquerque, New Mexico. I nailed some plywood over the broken window part, and we left town for about six days. We came back home, got repair estimates from three places, and called the insurance company. In a short period of time, we received a check for you won't believe this-$3,000! We got some beautiful French doors for that amount. All I had to do was to stain them! Once again God had made known his victory number of three (3) (Luke 24:7).

A Great Fire in the Mountain

I received another dream from the Lord on May 5, 2008—the *fifth (5)* day of the *fifth (5)* month, which was a double dose of grace (Isa. 9:6; Eph. 4:11). This was a continuation of the dream from July 6, or 7/6, which I now know to be the downfall of the stock market, the housing bubble, and other things. This dream came in the *seventh (7)* month, which was God's number. I believe He was saying that He was judging this country on its works.

Of course, sin is always involved. According to 1 Corinthians 3:12–15, even a Christian's works can be burned when God's great fire of judgment comes. In this dream, a great fire was burning down everything in its path, and we could see it coming toward our house! It had already destroyed many homes and businesses of all kinds. The fire was in the mountains.

We made sure that everyone was out of the house, for every family member was at my house. I told my wife that I was going to get a water hose and try to keep the house wet until the fire department arrived. The fire was about five stories high and full of smoke. I could feel the heat from the fire.

I believe God was saying that I would feel the effects and that my works and some of my finances would be tested by His fire of judgment. However, nothing serious happened.

By the time my wife had advised me not to challenge this fiery monster, it had jumped over the house, burned some evergreens, and gone down the mountain about a quarter of a mile and continued to burn. As superheroes were diving in and out of the earth, my wife made a statement that no man could stop this great fire. We finally realized that this was no ordinary fire.

A Great Fire in the Plains

On August 27, 2008, I had a final dream of this great fire. We were in a house on the plains, no longer in the mountains. We again observed a great fire. I told everyone to get any money they had and leave. Some people were hesitant about leaving, and they stood by a large glass window. I told them that the heat from the fire would break the glass and they would be harmed by it. I remembered the last fire, which had been in the mountains. It finally came to my mind that the fire was now on the plains in Las Vegas!

In both dreams, we could feel the fire. I also noticed that my house on the plains was not as glamorous as it had been in the mountains. We drove away in a style like the Beverly Hillbillies, with people hanging on to every side of our automobile. I never did see the house burn, because in real life the Lord had already told me to pay off the house. Through the dream, the Lord was telling me what was and what would be. He allowed me to feel the heat of the fire, because everyone would feel the terrible downfall of the economy and the housing bubble. The fire was now in the desert, which was Las Vegas. We were the last ones to feel it!

The dream was a warning to get our money if we had any. In other words, the value of our house was falling fast. That was the reason we got our money and left so quickly and so poor! The *eighth* (8) month was the beginning of something that Las Vegas had never experienced in my lifetime. The *twenty-seventh (27)* day involves the number *two* (2) the witness number (Rev. 11:3) and *seven (7)*, God's number. On the *seventh* (7) day, God rested (Gen. 2:2; Lev. 23:6). There are also the *seven* (7) days of unleavened bread. The year was 2008. I believe that God was telling me, as the interpretation read out, that this was his judgment on the United States. There are no coincidences with God. There was no insurance in the dream, because the only insurance is obedience.

There have been other dreams, and I have interpreted most of them right, but sometimes I miss what God is saying. The Dow Jones closed October 29. October is the *tenth (10)* month, which is the Bible's number of completeness and perfection (Gen. 16:3). The stock market was down by $777.68 billion. There was also a *seven (7)* -billion-dollar bailout. On 2/17/09, President

Obama signed a stimulus package of $787 billion. Notice all the sevens (7) which adds up to be seven (7)!

The number *two (2)* (for February, the second (2) month) and *seventeen (17)* (for the seventeenth day) indicated that God was saying, "You are witnesses to my judgment" (Rev. 11:3)! Those were all God's numbers. It was no coincidence. On September 28, 2008, which was a month before the stock market fell, I received a dream from the Lord. Other people, as well as my wife and myself, noticed a police officer and signs on our side of the road, and we were ordered to turn around. There was a great flood of water coming our way.

I turned around, expecting to get hit by the great flood, but I never did! I also noticed the gloom of the day. You see, God will continue to warn those who have a relationship with Him, those who have ears to hear. This time His judgment came as a great flood, but it was the same judgment and warning as the fire.

God will meet you where you are. The police officer was the Holy Spirit. I call the Holy Spirit the police of the universe, because He is omnipresent (everywhere). God was also saying that the doom and gloom of the weather was indicative of the times. All people who were not operating within God's will would have a spirit of fear. Amos 3:7 says that God never does anything without his servants, the prophets. I believe that I am also in the office of a prophet.

CHAPTER 4

Death of a Wonderful Pastor

Pastor Jackson died of cancer on his *fifty-seventh* (57) birthday. He was six feet tall and weighed two hundred pounds, but when he died, he was only a shell of himself. The irony is that the day of Pastor Jackson's death was also our grandson J. P.'s seventh (7) birthday. Earlier I said that our son Joseph died on my brother's Willie's birthday. It was a sad day at the *third (3)* church. It happened so quickly that we weren't prepared for it. Pastor Jackson's final number was *fifty-seven (57)* years, and I hope those numbers were God's way of saying, "by my grace and by my will."

The pastor's presence was greatly missed, we agreed that we would vote on whether to go to one of the other churches our pastor had come from or to vote for one of our elders to be the new pastor. Three of us voted for another pastor, and four of us voted for the elder to be promoted. In retrospect, I realize that I was the odd person who didn't really know or have anything to lose or gain. Each person had come from California except for one. But even he knew more about the elder than I thought I did.

The irony was that I was the deciding factor, and I was the one sitting in the *seventh (7)* chair! My vote changed everything. I believe the Lord's will and purpose for that church was for training certain people, myself included. I learned something from Pastor Jackson and others that he invited to the church. It wasn't long before the whole church was split in half. They knew that by voting in the elder as the new pastor, everything would change for the worst. Those who had been under my teaching at the Bible study left. The new pastor discontinued the Bible study, and all the other elders left as well. So I was ordained as an elder and left my position as a deacon.

There were two men who wanted to take matters into their own hands. I warned them that the Lord was in control and that this was the Lord's church and they would be judged for their actions. It was no coincidence that it was communion Sunday, the *seventh (7)* day of the *fifth (5)* month (may seventh), when these two guys arrived in the middle of service and allowed the spirit of Satan to control their flesh. They called the police, but they finally left. Before leaving, they made some strong accusations about the new pastor to his face. I didn't really know if these things were true or false. That evening, my wife and I weren't sure what was true.

Realizing that I was part of the situation, we went before the Lord that night and the words of the Lord came to me. He said, "You got the low-down, dirty truth!" God gave me another dream, and he said, "He's straight but not straight!" God also told me the title of a new book. The Lord was saying that, although he did not approve of the way the accusations had been made, they were the truth! That truth also would be confirmed by the true colors of the new pastor. He look and sound straight, but, not straight. Even my wife received confirmation about things we knew to be true, things that only a few of us in the leadership knew.

My authority as an elder was soon taken from me. Prayer was given to me, already worded and prepared, which was not scriptural. The Lord continued to talk to me about the situation as time went by. My wife and I were no longer happy there, and I began to tell the Lord that I wanted to leave that church. I could feel the difference, the Spirit of God was no longer in control. Time had been made available for my wife and I to leave.

One Saturday night when I got off work early, the Lord gave me a plan. We executed it the very next morning, which was Sunday. My wife and I felt like we had been released from prison. Praise God! We had been under this pastor for a whole year, but it felt like two. After *eight* (8) years, the number of new beginning (Gen. 21:4), we were looking forward to a new beginning! It was also the month of March the *third (3)* month, the victory number.

God is a big God, but He is a little-by-little God for our benefit (Deut. 7:20–23). The love that we had once enjoyed in that church was gone.

A Variety of Different Churches

From that point on, we visited churches and watched a lot of ministries on TV. We eventually joined another church before we came to the one we are at now. My wife and I went to the Lord on the last church, as we did with all the churches. There was always something that the Lord wanted us to learn at the church he sent us to: to discern the good and the bad, to observe the mistakes as part of our experiences of the church. Sometimes, we were there to assist and support the pastor or to give a special offering to that church. We were to be a blessing, to give a word.

We did have an experience at another church that is worth mentioning. We were invited to come to the church to pray for the church, direction and other things. I was not able to go because of work hours. However, Pat went on two occasions but did not enjoy the prayer event. She said, that she experienced some type of weird headache. She was later invited again. For a while she was hesitant to go, but on a later occasion, she talked herself into going once more. She reasoned that her headache had probably been the result of a long day at work, or something to that effect. She came home more concerned than before.

She said that she'd not only gotten a headache but had also seen a dark hole! We continued to go to the church, but we never participated in the prayer event.

I received a word and a dream from the Lord regarding the church. The dream I received from the Lord was very vivid. It involved a very big building that was very dark, with the exception of a small light in the rear. I knew in the dream that the heads of the church and the denomination were there in this small room, meeting or socializing. For some reason, the Lord had given me the gift of discernment. I had already warned the leaders that someone or something was coming and had told them to be vigilant to the wiles of the Devil. But my words had fallen on deaf ears.

It was a full moon that night in the dream (2 King 4:22-23), which itself speaks of prophecy. Also in the dream, I was watching the door, but I didn't know whom I was watching for. No doubt I was a watchman for the Lord. Those who are in the fivefold ministry must be God's watchmen (Isa. 21:8-9). As I was watching the door, angels came in looking like ninjas. I screamed to the leaders in the back room, "They're here! They're here!" I could barely see them in the light of the full moon, as they disappeared in the shadows of darkness. They had bows and arrows in hand. I thought they were going to shoot me, but they hadn't been sent to harm me. I continue to scream in terror as I woke up!

This was no doubt a dream from the Lord. He allowed me to see from the spirit world the thing that he was about to do. He knew that I was displeased with the situation at the church. Death angels had been sent to this church. Only God would write the final chapter. These death angels reminded me of the angel that had killed 185,000 Assyrians in one night! (2 Kings 19:35). If that wasn't enough to frighten us away from the church, the next event would.

One Saturday after an event on the *seventh* (7) day, we came home just before dusk. We settled down in the kitchen with our backs turned away from the entrance and the front doors. We had no lights on in the kitchen, for the entry lights came on at dusk and lit up the whole entrance and the large living room area. We were sitting slightly in the dark, but we had not yet closed the patio blinds. Therefore, the patio glass doors mirrored the entryway.

As we sat in the slightly dark kitchen having a conversation, we noticed a figure in the hallway going the opposite way down the hallway steps! We looked at each other in shock and asked each other, "Did you see that?" We got up and went in that direction, turning on all the lights in the back rooms, as if we were going to see something. We searched all the rooms but found nothing. My wife wanted to use the reflection of the TV as an explanation. I insisted that in all the years we had been in the house, we had never had any kind of reflection.

We finally came to the conclusion that we had just seen our first spirit of some kind! We thought about it, and I realized that we had just come from the church, and this thing had followed us home! We went into every room, casting out this thing, this foul spirit, from our house in the name of Jesus, by His blood, by the cross, in His mighty name and in righteous indignation, as in Matthew 21:12. We had the great authority of Jesus. We also anointed each entrance way with oil.

Although we were invited back to that church, we never went. We got the Lord's message that he wanted us to stay clear of that place, because his judgment was coming. The prominence of the church and its leaders were not the same. Right away we could see the judgment of God!

It wasn't long before the Lord showed me in a dream that I was teaching in a certain part of town, an area where a friend lived. Also, a new church was being built, enabling us to start our involvement on the ground floor. The Lord spoke to my wife in a dream as well. Pastor Jackson, our old pastor from the third (3) church, was standing on the new property when we drove by, and he asked her if she was going to the new church. That was our *second* confirmation, and *two (2)* is God's witness number.

Behind Door Number 5

God's grace is amazing (2 Cor. 12:9). In the month of May, the *fifth* (5) month, which is the month of grace,

God gave me an experience behind door number *five (5)*. It was a homosexual experience, but there were no males or females and no body parts involved! God gave me a mental experience of homosexuality for his own reasons. It was like a dream of having a sexual experience with the opposite sex, but instead it was a rectal experience. I must make it clear, make it known, and make a notation that I have never in my life had or desired that kind of experience. It took me five years or more before I could tell my wife about the experience. I kept asking the Lord why he had given me this experience.

From the time I had the experience it stayed in my head and I asked the Lord to take it away. I read a book years ago called *A Divine Revelation from Hell*. In this book, the Lord Jesus took a dedicated Christian woman out of her body and took her to hell. She was allowed to see the terrible suffering, sorrow, pain, and loneliness. The Lord also left her there alone, and she cried out for him, thinking He had left her there, not intending to return. He finally came back to get her after only thirty minutes, but it had seemed like an eternity! She was so thankful and grateful. She thought about those poor souls who would be there forever. The Lord told her He had not liked leaving her there, but the experience would be helpful for her ministry and walk with Christ. From that point on, she said she had a totally different view of salvation and hell.

This was what the Lord wanted me to experience. He wanted me to recognize that homosexuality was something a person could get trapped in, a lifestyle of sorts. It could affect people who had been molested as children and people who had homosexual desires. Some desires, whatever they might be, are a consequence of the fall of man and the resulting curse. Caught up in Satan's lie, many people believe they were made that way. Perhaps this is true, to a point, but we must make adjustments as we do with anything else. An all-loving God would never ask us to do something that we are not capable of doing through the cross and the Holy Spirit.

Someone told my wife that her own daughter had revealed that she was a lesbian. The mother had responded by saying, "You know you're going to hell, don't you?" Well, that was not quite right. We are all heading in that direction if we don't receive Jesus (Prov. 14:32). It wouldn't matter if a person had never sinned before in his life. You see, we are born into sin. We were contaminated by Adam, our federal head (1 Cor. 15:22). Unless we receive Jesus the second man and the last Adam—we are lost (1 Cor. 15:45–49). Notice that this verse uses the phrase "the *last* Adam," meaning that there will be no need for another. Just before his last breath, Jesus said, "It is finished!"

The Lord was saying that I had to have that experience for several reasons: (1) I was very critical of the homosexual lifestyle, although I loved the people involved in it; (2) it opened my understanding of how a person can get caught up in that lifestyle; (3) it made me aware that most people don't know how to get out of the lifestyle; and (4) God showed me that there is a way out of this lifestyle. It's all about trusting Jesus and his finished work on the cross, praying, and waiting. The law that operates it is powerful because of the weakness of the flesh (Rom. 8:1–2). It is so easy to say, "It is my civil right to get married as a gay couple." A drunk has the right to get drunk in his or her home, but it is not right in the eyes of God, which supersedes man's law.

The homosexual experience calls for desperate measures. The Lord allowed me the experience, because He knew He had already given me the way out of it and the ability to counsel others. The Lord told me that His grace was sufficient for me, for His strength was made perfect in my weakness (2 Cor. 12:9). I could say, as the apostle Paul did, that I had a thorn in the flesh. Jesus was the only way out of that lifestyle, that sin. Although I had never lived the homosexual lifestyle, I understood from the experience the Lord gave me that it was like a mind-controlling drug. From what the Lord showed me, it was a sin that made me feel perverted and dirty. But I had felt the powerful control of the experience, and the weakness of the flesh. In that situation, it wouldn't matter how a person's loved ones or parents felt, because most parents disowned that lifestyle anyway.

I thank the Lord for showing me the experience so that he might send a few homosexuals my way. I am saved by the blood of Jesus, and the Lord gave me the victory by my understanding of the cross. But if I didn't know Christ or have an understanding of the cross, who knows what would have happened in my life? I prayed, "Lord, take this thing away from me. Take it away from my thoughts. Lord, I know that I am in you, in your finished work, in your perfect rest, identified with and positioned in you, Lord Jesus. You and the cross are the object of my faith, the cross being the means, and you, Lord Jesus, being the source." It wasn't long before I could feel the pressure of this thing leaving me, and after a while, only the faded memory of it stayed. Praise God! It was just like the experience of the woman who had been taken to hell.

If you don't know Christ, I ask you now to come to Jesus. He will meet you where you are. Say this prayer: "God, I am a sinner. I am lost, and I need your Son, Jesus, to come into my life to be my Lord and Savior. Then I will no longer be a lost son of Adam, but a son of the heavenly Father. In Jesus' name, amen." If you prayed this prayer, you are now a new creation. Old things are passed away, and behold, all things have become new (2 Cor. 5:17).

Dreams of Retirement

It was April or May. I am not sure of the month, but I am sure of the date. It was the *seventh (7)* day of the month when I received a vivid dream from the Lord. In my dream, I received a piece of paper from a person on my job. The paper said that I had paid my dues. I had paid something off! As I was driving home in my Cadillac

Seville, I felt great joy, expecting to cry at any time, but I never did. As I drove home, I noticed *two (2)* persons who looked like women I knew from somewhere. Perhaps they were relatives. Each had a water hose in hands and was watering the lawn, it was green everywhere. I also noticed that the house was sitting on a very high hill, so high that I had to turn the wheels of the car opposite the incline of the hill (Matt. 7:24–27). I once had a word from the Lord and He said "follow the green grass." Perhaps He was saying: "observe the green grass,' we must watch the grass to keep it green and healthy, watering it with water as we do with the Holy Spirit, we must weed and feed it with the word which is the Bible; basic instructions before leaving earth. And allow the Holy Spirit to weed out the things He do not want in our life. We must allow Him to trim and cut us back for better and stronger growth. This is perhaps what I believe the Holy Spirit was showing me through the angels with the water hoses, as they kept everything green, healthy and prosperous.

God's number *seven (7)* was total and complete in my life and my job (Ps. 12:6). With God, there is no easy way out, not in this sense. He was saying that I had paid my dues, and my time had come for retirement, at least the physical vocation. As these things were revealed to me, I felt great joy. I don't know why I didn't cry. I believe that the *two* people who were watering the lawn were also my wife's and my angels.

Here is another revelation: the *two (2)* angels refer to the number of witnesses (Rev. 11:3). Along with myself, we equaled *three (3)*, which is the victory number (Gen. 41:46). Joseph was *thirty* (30) years old, after being in slavery and the dungeon for *thirteen (13)* years. We have God's *seven* (7) and the *three (3)* in thirty. Praise God!

I also believe that God was saying that the *two (2)* angels were assisting my wife and I in the Lord's business and were helping to bless us. Hence, everything was green. The fence and gates represented His angels encamped around us (Ps. 34:6–8; Matt. 7:24–27). He was saying that I was a wise man, meaning that I had built my house on a rock, not sand, which enabled me to retire early. Praise God

The Faith of a Gentile Woman

A couple came to the hotel one day, and I served them with food and conversation. They asked me, what I was going to do in retirement. I proceeded to tell them, I was getting involved with the church. I also told them about other spiritual things as well. They were very encouraged. It wasn't long after I'd talked to them that they received faith.

The lady gave me a note, but I didn't read it until I got home. The note read something like this: "James, would you please pray for my daughter Bonnie Jean and my grandchildren? She has a problem forgiving, and I haven't seen her in *five (5)* years. I love her deeply. Pray that she comes home to Mom soon. Thank you. Jean." I still have the note. I saw the number *five (5)* on the note, and I reminded the Lord about his grace. I prayed for Jean's prayer to come true and continued to intercede.

After a period of time, I was at work one evening. As I was passing by a table, I heard my name called out. It was that same lady Jean and her husband. She asked me where had I been and said they had been looking for me. I responded by saying that I had been there all along. She was excited; I could see it in her face. She said that her daughter had called her after (5) *five* years and that she was coming to visit. I don't believe this lady knew the Lord, because the business card on which she'd written her note was not Christ like. I was not judging her, but observing she had more faith than some believers (Matt. 15:21–28).

A Shocking Biopsy Report

In 2009 the year of fourfold grace, I received a biopsy that revealed that I had prostate cancer. It came out of nowhere, with no warning, but the Lord gave me His peace within the storm. Praise God. Also, my dear wife was there, as always. This is the letter she wrote to me while I was asleep in bed. She left it on the table on her way to work. It was so helpful.

She wrote: "Hi, Honey, Just a note to let you know how much I love you, and to let you know that we are in this together. The Lord takes us through trials, but he never gives us more than we can bear. We will be prayerful and continue to follow Him and stand on His promises."

Your loving wife, Pat.

I made an appointment with the oncologist after confirming with the urologist a decision on how to treat it. The bittersweet news was that my chances were great. He said that (1) I had good health and no major problems and (2) a good frame of mind (I responded that these things were Jesus' doing), (3) longevity in the family's history, and (4) an early diagnosis. We came up with a treatment of radiation, and each treatment only lasted for about *three (3)* minutes, which was the victory number. It would take forty-four (44) days which is the complete number of creation. The first treatment started on 1/14/10, which was a Thursday, the *fifth (5)* day of the week, the day of grace. *Ten (10)* was the number of perfection and completeness in the Bible. Also, I had a dream right after the biopsy report on a Thursday night to Friday morning.

A Visit from the Lord

I always look at the clock after having a dream from the Lord. It was *three (3)* a.m the victory number. The dream was so vivid and real! The first thing I remembered about it was that someone had pointed out a large crowd of people about a mile away. We were all in a desert-like place, and the sand was as white as snow. There were two (2) others with Him, making them *three (3)*. It was as if the Lord was saying, "I brought the victory number." I remembered the voice of a person asking me, "Do you see all those people there?" I said yes. I understood that the person speaking was the Lord Jesus, although I did not see His face.

I didn't see the faces of His two companions either, but I came to the conclusion that they were the same two angels who had accompanied the Lord when He visited Abraham and Sarah (Gen. 18:1–2)! They stood by His side as the Lord was speaking. He told me that those people wouldn't need their shoes or clothes, for they would die in the army of the Lord! "You will wear their shoes and clothes!" He said.

About that time I felt the Lord was no longer there, I was alone. Then something came out of the ground, missing my foot by an inch or two. They were about the size of a small steam iron. They had tails about the size of a lead pencil. In color, they were reddish-orange and gray, like wood coals. Something like this would come to the earth during the great tribulation period, but it won't be a dream!

I was told that these things were foot-eaters. I figured out on my own that I would die if they got ahold of my foot!

As time went by, I was given the ability to discern their presence, to see them while they were still underground. When they came up, they were *ten (10)* feet away, the number of completeness. Proverbs 3:25–26 says, "Be not afraid of sudden fear, neither of the desolation of the wicked, when it cometh. For the Lord shall be thy confidence, and shall keep thy foot from being taken."

God had given me the victory number over prostate cancer. Praise God! Hallelujah!

CHAPTER 5

God Had Already Planned Everything

Before my treatment was acknowledged, management at work decided to change our days off so they could maximize our workforce. We usually did everything by seniority. I was the first one on the list if they went by *room* seniority, but I was *fifth (5)* if they went by *house*, which they did. I should have known that God was in the number *five (5)* (Rev. 9:5). Before they came up with the new system, I had Sunday and Monday off. By the time they got to me, there was no Sunday/Monday left, nor Saturday/Sunday.

However, the days that the Lord wanted me to have off were Friday/Saturday. All the time I had worked there, I never had those days off. The reason being, they were two of the busiest days of the week. Later, as I was diagnosed with prostate cancer and received my treatment, I was very thankful for my new schedule. I had already had a powerful dream from the Lord, which gave me unshakeable faith.

The Lord allows us to be tried and tested for our good (1 Cor. 10:13), but the Devil comes to steal, kill, and destroy (John 10:10). Let me take us back in time to Pamper, Texas, when I was only *twenty-three (23)* (my number), and the Lord was teaching me how to be a man. At that time, my number was not so friendly. Actually, the whole year was not friendly, for God will protect us only for so long when we are wrong.

I had a dream from the adversary: I was carrying my wife on my back, when I was bitten by a viper. Afterward, I mentioned the dream to an old lady I knew. The first thing she asked me was, "Did you kill the snake?" I said no. She said, "If you don't kill the snake in a dream, it means that your enemy will overcome you!" About a few weeks later, I was stabbed with a knife! That was a different world then.

But Satan will try everything. My faith would take me back to the Scriptures, to Acts 28:3–4. Paul was gathering firewood, when he was bitten by a viper of the most dangerous kind. But Paul not only had great faith, he had the Scriptures (2 Cor. 12:9), which supersede everything! His grace is sufficient for me: for his strength is made perfect in my weakness. Also, Paul had God's promise that he would be brought before Caesar (Acts 27:23–24).

February 14 was my worst day at work, as the radiation treatments were starting to take their toll. During the last month of radiation, after a certain day, which was Sunday, the treatments began to burn. Having experienced this burning the previous times, I decided to take off from work the rest of the Sundays. The experience was terrible, and I had to run to the restroom every ten minutes with a terrible burning sensation. On top of that, I had a long night at work. The Lord allowed Satan to try me by fire that night. God's number *seven (7)* was present, along with the time I got home, which was 12:35 a.m. The numbers indicates conclusion with grace.

That night, Satan himself sent a party into our restaurant. I continued to burn as the customers continued to make it hard for me. Finally, they all asked for separate checks, and they were now in a hurry. It took me forever to get the checks right. The truth was that, although I had some help from buddy boy Hugo, we never did get those checks quite right. The other bad news was that they all got up at once, and money was everywhere, but they shorted me by *forty (40)* dollars! This was the number for probation as well as rest, but I felt that this one meant probation. But I stayed focused on Jesus, for I am and I was positioned in Him Praise God!

Genesis 19:9 says, "And the Lord said unto him, take me a heifer of three (3) years old and a she goat of three (3) years old, and a ram of three (3) years old, and a turtledove and a pigeon." Notice the threes of these animals, the number for victory. After what I had been through in 2010 with the treatment and the job, the Lord knew that I needed some kind of confirmation. If the great apostle Paul needed some assurance (Acts 23:11), so do we all.

In our *thirty-fifth (35)* year, there were *five (5)* of us that had survived to celebrate. I know that God protected me all the time, and He blessed the restaurant as well. As Christians, we must realize that we, through the Lord, are the salt and the light to those around us. There was a time when a certain problem came about among my fellow employees and the maître d'. At that time, I was not as mature in Christ as I am now and even now I have not arrived, for God is not finished with me yet. I worked with an older person who had a very profane and intimidating mouth. We had a disagreement one time, and I was called to the maître d's office, and from there to the top food and beverage office. I had no time to tell my side of the story before I was hauled upstairs.

These bosses were from Chicago. When one of them got through threatening me, I was afraid that I would lose my job. Even my maître d' felt sorry for me. One particular guy really took the situation personally. He would come through the restaurant just to harass me. It wasn't long before my heavenly Father made a judgment on them. The whole group was fired! Judgment starts at home (1 Peter 4:17), but they never knew what hit them! The Lord is a righteous God. Praise Him! Glorify His name!

I feel very grateful to the Lord for leading me into retirement. In retrospect, I am very thankful that the Lord chose the right maître d' and management for our room. Each person was sent to our room when we needed them the most. The maître d' from New York was in the room when I went in there. A host of managers worked in our room as maître d', but only *five (5)* were there for any length of time, which was the number of grace. For example, Mario the Cuban, the Lord had him in the room when I was going through my divorce, and for reasons I won't mention, he was the right manager for me at that time. Praise God. The other managers were Eric, Mario W., and Ilario. It was a pleasure to work for and with all of them.

When I retired, I was the employee who had been in the room the longest, although I was not the oldest in the room. Two employees were eleven and twelve years older than myself. After I retired, Sister Agnes and maître d' Ilario followed suit, after seeing that the waters of retirement were safe. The Lord told me He had a calling on my life, and everything I'd experienced since the day I was born had been preparation. Someone had told me years ago that I would be a Moses, in the sense of being used at an older age. Moses' life had *three (3)* parts to it. For his first *forty (40)* years, he was raised and educated in Egyptian culture, which was one of the most intellectual systems at that time. During the second *forty (40)* years, God humbled Moses in the desert, removing Egypt from him through humility. He was now fit and ready to serve. It was his *third (3)* – forty (40) years that gave him the victory.

God is no respecter of persons (2 Chron. 19:7). As I examine my life, I see a pattern there. I was not raised as an Egyptian and did not have that type of education. I was not called to lead the Jews out of Egypt or to write five books of the Bible—six, if you count Job, which some people believe Moses wrote. Moses and I both was run out of town. We both was chased into the desert. Him being the back of the desert, me being the desert of Las Vegas. Two parts of my life also were preparation. Moses got victory in the *third (3)* segment of his life, and he was *eighty (80)* when he received his calling, which is the number of new beginning. Joe Haldeman-an American science fiction author. He also wrote – All My Sins Remembered, as well as Star Trek. He said the life of Moses presents a series of striking antitheses. For instance, he was a child of a slave and the son of a queen. He was born in a hut and lived in a palace. He inherited poverty and enjoyed unlimited wealth. He was the leader of armies and the keeper of flocks. He was the mightiest of warriors and the meekest of men. He was educated in the court of Egypt, yet he dwelt in the desert. He had the wisdom of Egypt and the faith of a child. He was fitted for the city and wandered in the wilderness. He was tempted with the pleasures of sin and endured the hardships of virtue. He was backward in speech, and yet he talked with God. He had the rod of a shepherd and the power of the infinite. He was a fugitive from Pharaoh and an ambassador from heaven. He was a giver of the Law and the forerunner of grace.

Are you in the back of a desert as Moses was? Sometimes we think God has forgotten us, that we will live the rest of our lives working at a meaningless job. But God has a better plan for us, if we answer his call. For a period of time, my wife and I had no church that we could call our own. We had lost touch with everyone in the *third* (3) church. It was as if we were in the back of the desert as well. The Lord gave me *three (3)* words one night, and God's numbers, combined with my number, were victory to me: 7/23/07. The words were "the forgotten dean." The Lord was saying, I have total and completeness in your life. He was letting me know that I was not forgotten. Praise Him.

Moses was *eighty (80)*, and David was the *eighth (8)* son, no doubt thinking he would always be a shepherd of sheep and not a shepherd of men as God's first chosen king (1 Sam. 16:10).

I believe God will give me victory in the *third* (3) part of my life. On 7/23 of this year, I will have been in the desert of Las Vegas for *forty (40)* years! The Lord spoke three (3) numbers to me the other night: *three (3), five (5)*, and *six (6)*. The words to those numbers were "victory by grace to man." Like Moses, I have been greatly humbled in my life. Humility comes before honor (Prov. 15:33). What kept me from getting impatient or getting ahead of God these last few years was the relationship I have and had with Him. He has told me some amazing things! Believe it or not, He even told me some things about politics that came true. He has given me many promises, but there is one that I will never forget.

My Name Called Out

Some years ago, as I was between sleeping and waking, between unconsciousness and consciousness, I heard my name being called: "James, James." I woke up, still half-asleep, wondering whether I had been dreaming or had only imagined someone calling my name. I mentioned it to my wife, but I don't remember her reply. I had been born under the name Jimmy, not James. In 1985 I changed my name at the Social Security office from Jimmy to James, because in all my credit and business affairs, I was called and known as James. Later, I had it done in totality. The number *eighty-five (85)* is the beginning of grace (Gen. 8:15-18; Sam.17:40).

I have said that to say this: I believe that the Lord dealt with my heart to change my name. Abraham and Paul had been born with names different from what God eventually called them. Abraham had been Abram (Gen. 17:5), and Paul had been Saul. The name Jimmy is not in the Bible, but James is. James is also the English equivalent of Jacob.

Two days after the dream, we went out of town and stayed on the *fourteenth* (14) or *seventeenth* (17) floor; it was one or the other. I remember that the number was God's number (Ps. 12:6; Rom. 11:4), whether it was *fourteen (14),* which is two sevens (7) (Elohim), or one (7) *seven.* Jesus is the one who called me that night, just as he had called Moses, and Saul.

As I was saying, that night on that particular floor, my name was called again, "James, James." From that point, I began to have a vivid dream. I was in the Cadillac Seville, and two evil characters were following me. They had the complexions of people of Middle Eastern descent. The next thing I knew, they were pushing me into some gas pumps, and I was helpless to do anything, so I braced myself for the explosion. There was a great explosion that blew me into kingdom come. I remember not feeling anything. It was like hitting my toe on a bedpost and expecting to feel great pain, but it never came. I was surrounded by brilliant light that was not of this world.

A few years later, I would read something from an edition of the *Old Farmer's Almanac* that was a witness to my dream In (John 12:23–24). This vivid dream took place on the street right across from West 2300 Bonanza Street, the street where I met my wife and other significant things happened.

A Visit from a Dead Aunt

At *eight* (8) o'clock on a Friday morning, which was the number of beginning, I had a dream about my dead Aunt Joyce. In this vivid dream, she looked even better than she had looked in the early years of her life when she was young and beautiful. In the dream, I said to myself, "She's dead. There's no need to follow her. She would only disappear." And she surely did.

The Lord was telling me that my dead aunt did not hang around, because it wasn't my time, thank God. I read in a book about hospice patients, that if your loved ones started to hang around your bed, your time was getting very close. On the *eighteenth* (18) day of March, the *third (3)* month, on a Monday morning, I had another dream about my dead Aunt Joyce. When I opened the door in the dream, she didn't say anything, but she came into the house and looked in two directions and left. I noticed that this time she was older than she had been in the first dream. I believe that the next time I see her, it will be my time to go away, just as the words were spoken to me. I believe she will look like a dead person the next time.

The Lord told me that my calling would last twenty-two years or more before I go away. Also, that day was the *eighteenth (18)*, which would indicate the beginning of my calling. My aunt Joyce was the *seventh (7)* child among my mother's siblings. I believe that is the reason she was the one sent. Some years ago, I knew a sister in Christ, who I believe was a prophetess. She told my wife and I, she had seen me preaching. Later she asked me and my wife if we were leaving the church, something that would actually take place about two to three years later. At the time, we responded by saying no. Later, she would die after being hit by a car as she was walking.

God Spoke the Number Forty

The Hebrew word *shagat* (pronounced *shaw-kat*) means "free from disturbance or turmoil, quiet, rest, idleness, settled, still" (Judg. 5:31; 8:28; Isa. 30:15; 32:17). While we rest, God prepares us. In this dream, the Lord spoke the number *forty (40)*. As I came out of the front door with a palm tree, He told me that *three (3)* was enough. Palm trees represent perfect rest and perfect climate (2 Chron. 3:05).

Here we have the number *three (3)*, which is the victory number. The amazing thing about the situation was this: God planted those *three (3)* palm trees without my assistance one up front and two in the backyard. Actually, everything about the house consisted of threes (3). There are three (3) gates on the property, a three (3)-car garage, three (3) patio doors, three (3) skylights, three (3) bathrooms, three (3) bedrooms, and three (3) levels. No wonder there was a three (3) in our address (1301). A major part of my life has been the number three (3). No wonder the number *twenty-three (23)* is in my life. The number *two (2)* is to witness the victory number *three (3)*.

To witness the number three (3) is to witness God, being three (3) in one (1). Another verse is to be acknowledged in the number three (3), we have victory over death, Hell, and the grave (Rom. 6:4-5). Praise God! Thank you Jesus!

Retirement

The *thirtieth* (30) day of the *twelfth (12)* month of 2010 was my last day at work. It was the fifth (5) day of the week Thursday, the day of grace. Being the *twelfth* (12) month, which is God's government number, it was as if Jesus was saying, I must be about the Father's business. At noon (Jn. 4:6; Mk.15:33:26:13) at midnight (Acts 16:25 20:7-12) "God showed His power and grace; before a shipwreck, God spoke to Paul (Acts 27:27-33). The year, being *ten (10)*, was the Bible's number for completeness. The *thirtieth (30)* day represents the victory that God gave me.

I was asked to come back on Tuesday to make my retirement official: to sign the papers, turn in company property, clean out my locker, and get my final payroll check. And by the way, that Tuesday was the *third (3)* day of the week. You can't make this stuff up. I left my *third* (3) job for the last time, and everything happened just as my dream had foretold!

Seven Holes in the House

We are instructed by the Lord to rest and to have the victory. Matthew 11:28–30 says, "Come unto me, all who labor and are heavy laden, and I will give you rest. Take my yoke upon you and learn of me; for I am meek and lowly in heart: and you shall find rest unto your souls. For my yoke is easy, and my burden is light." It's all about the cross. We must learn of Christ, for his sacrifice is for our benefit. We must rest in what he has already done.

One night I had a very vivid dream. I was riding a bike from the side of the house to the back, when I noticed someone very close to me, riding on the same bike. I believed it to be the Holy Spirit. As we proceeded to the back of the house, I saw a fountain of water coming from the foundations of my home and the backyard wall. What bothered me most was that the water was muddy, which was a sign of trouble. A word also came to me from the Lord: *sacrifice*. I told my wife about it and told her to brace herself, for something big was about to happen.

My daughter Laritta called me. She had been instructed to call everyone in the family at least those who were close. Along with a word from the Lord, she'd had a dream. In her dream, she had come to the house while I was outside washing the car. She stood at the gate, calling to me, but I couldn't hear her. It was those two warnings that had provoked her to call me. She was the only one God had informed of what had already happened. I believe the Lord needed only one other person to make it *three (3)*, the victory number. Laritta would be that third (3) person to pray, to intercede, to stand in the gap and pray a hedge around us. Praise God.

As I looked back on my own dream, I said, "The Holy Spirit was riding on the back of my bike, saying that he had my back, that he wouldn't leave me or forsake me. Praise God." The dream came on a Tuesday, the *third* (3) day (victory), on the *seventeenth (17)* day of the month. God's number of completeness and perfection was there (Gen.41:18).

On a Sunday after church (July 15, 2012), I noticed that the sink was stopped up. I tried everything I could to unstop it, but to no avail. We finally called the plumber out, after praying about which company to call. The first guy came out with a snake and ran it about fifty feet under the house, but the sink was still stopped up. He finally called the other guy out with a camera, and he ran the camera about a hundred or so feet. As I watched, he showed me the problem. He said that the pipes had come loose under the house and foundation, and there was raw sewage there!

To make a long story short, we were in for a very expensive job. If my memory serves me right, it was to cost about two hundred dollars a foot, starting at the kitchen, which was at the opposite end of the house. We would have to replace the sewage pipes in all the restrooms throughout the house and run the pipes all the way to the street, and it was a very long way to the main sewer. The price came to $42,000! We were shocked. It was a good thing that the Lord had warned us beforehand. I remembered telling my wife Pat about my dream. When God said "sacrifice," He meant sacrifice.

The lead workman, who was a believer himself, told us that he would give us a $7,000 break because we were Christians. That number alone (*seven*) (7) was God's number. The bad thing was that the cost was not covered by our homeowner's insurance. We received favor from the Lord, in that the insurance adjuster came out to look at the problem. We were able to get new tile in all the bathrooms, the kitchen, and the laundry room—not that we asked for it, but the adjuster insisted that we had it.

We ended up paying about $25,000 out of our pockets. The contractor said it would take about a week or so to do it, and they would only make holes where it was totally necessary. We were thankful that they used a special tool to keep from making holes all the way through the house. God is good all the time.

We told them to get started as soon as possible. I thanked the Lord that I had retired so I could be home and not worry about going to work. We started the work right away, but the Lord did not alert our daughter Laritta until the *twenty-third (23)*. It was about time that number showed up, but there was another *twenty-three (23)*. The house foundation had been built in 1989, and the problem occurred in 2012, *twenty-three* (23) years later. As I have said before, *twenty-three (23)* is not always a favorable number, but it is an experienced teacher.

The inspectors had let one thing slip by. I will comment more on that later. The noise was extremely loud, for they had to jackhammer the foundation. Dust flew everywhere. They had to carry the dirt from the foundation in buckets, in and out of the front door and rear windows. It was like a construction zone inside. We started out with a hole in each bathroom and one in the kitchen. Before it was over, we had a second hole in the kitchen and one in the master bedroom.

When they were not working, we had to cover the holes at night with plywood. We had so much dirt and dust in the house that it took my wife and I six months to finally make it dust-free again. A few years ago, I had a dream that it would be a rocky road to my calling. I'd never thought that our castle and home would be a part of that. Right before we built the house we had to make a choice on the sub-contractors. I had promised a plumber that I would hire him for the plumbing, but when the pressure came we made a decision to use someone else. I believe the Lord was not pleased with our choice. When your foundation is weak, sooner or later everything will come tumbling down. I believed the Lord allowed the inspector not to see the problem. It felt as though the mess and noise would never end, but we had our faith in the Lord. "My brethren, count it all joy when you fall into various trials, knowing that the testing of your faith produces patience. But let patience have its perfect work, that you might be perfect and complete, lacking nothing (James

1:3–4). After a period of *five* (5) weeks, the Lord's grace gave us peace (Rom. 1:7).

A Giant Serpent

I had a dream about a giant serpent. In the dream, I found myself in a house writing a book. It was also made known to me that my wife Pat was there. There was a *third (3)* person there as well, someone my wife and I knew very well. He could do anything, He had not failed in anything and we had total confidence and security in Him. I noticed that we had only one window in this place, but it was beginning to darken. As I watched, a giant serpent climb up the side of the building!

It was so huge that as it climbed the building which I believed to be our home it continued to take away the light. The *third (3)* person was no longer in the house. Instead, He was outside, ready to attack the giant serpent. This serpent began to speak, saying that he was coming after Pat. I realized that it was Satan, that old serpent who had come to deceive. When we are in Christ, we have everything. We're blessed going in and going out. When we walk in the spirit, not in the flesh, we are protected in every way. We have the Spirit of wisdom, which is also the law of the Spirit of life in Christ Jesus, who has made me free from the law of sin and death (Rom. 8:1–2). Because of that *third (3)* person, as well as the number *three (3)*, we will receive the victory in Christ, by God's will, every time. Praise God.

The Thirty-Fifth Year of the Cadillac Seville

After *thirty-five (35)* years of having the Seville (1978 to 2013), God allowed me to have a new automobile. We started this book with the number *thirty-five* (Highway 35), and now we are reminded of *thirty-five (35)* years again. I paid $14,723 for the Seville. It's amazing the numbers are there. They read: *fourteen (14)* (God the Father and God the Son), *seven (7)* (God the Holy Spirit), and *twenty-three (23)* (my number). We would witness God's victories thru that car in the conclusion of everything in our life. Without doubt, the car had been a total and complete car in my life for *thirty-five (35)* years. Perhaps it might die when I die, according to the dream!

I bought the Seville in the month of May, for no other month would fit the occasion. As I mentioned before, the license plate numbers was 556-BNC: "double grace to man, Before Not Christ like." The car, or a truckload of cars, had been ordered from Abilene (Luke: 3:1). I also purchased the license plates in May. However, when we went on strike, I drove on expired plates. The Lord allowed it until the first day we went back to work from the strike. As I was driving to work, a motorcycle policeman came out of nowhere and followed me into the employee's parking lot to give me a ticket. The officer was nice. He informed me that I could show proof of registration, and the judge would drop the citation.

In 2010, a few months before my retirement, I passed two police cars in the neighborhood. As I was driving home, the one police car had its lights on as it followed me into my driveway! I came out of the garage, and the officer told me that I was driving with expired plates. I couldn't believe it! But he was right. Someone had dropped the ball, and it wasn't me. Like clockwork, I had always received an expiration notice in the mail.

Nevertheless, this time God had something to do with it. It was three months over do, God's number of conclusion. I went the very next day and got my registration. I noticed that the registration date read 10/27/10. I received discernment and was enlightened: this was God's will for the Seville. In the Bible, *ten (10)* means perfection or completeness. With God's number two (2) and *seven (7)* in the middle He has allowed me to witness perfect and completeness in the car. He made this car to last from the beginning to the end. There was a *ten (10)* at the beginning and at the end of the date.

I received the 2013 Acura SUV-RDX in 2012 of ninth (9) month, His fourfold grace. I believe it to represent God's victory in and through me. The license plate number is 655-YKG. The amazing thing about this license plate is that the first *three* numbers are reversed and would read "man with double grace." The letters could read, "Yes, King God."

As God has given me the victory in cars, I also believe in the calling He has given me. In the year 2012, the *ninth* of October, we had a "Hope for the World" event, a local ministry service project. It started on a Tuesday night and ended on a Saturday afternoon. The idea was to participate in the ministry of one's choice. We chose to go that afternoon with Bob and Kathleen to the ministry called "Highway to Hope." We prepared lunch bags, served the homeless, and offered prayer and evangelism. The location this time was on Eighth and Fremont Street. As people came by, we offered them a burger, a Bible, and a bottle of water. We also asked if they needed salvation and/or prayer.

There was many different needs represented, such as the death of a loved one or kids being taken away from a mother, because she was hooked on drugs and alcohol. In general, people needed prayer. Finally, when we had given out everything, we came together in a circle of prayer. I believe Bob led us in prayer, as we were greatly aware of the Holy Spirit in the circle. At that time, under the spirit of anointing and conviction, we had one mind and one spirit, and it came to me to ask the Lord for divine revelation about where he was taking me and my wife in the ministry. God had not yet given me the burden to start this book. Notice the dates and the numbers: Saturday (the *seventh* day), October (the *tenth* month), and the *ninth (9)* day of the month 2012. In these numbers were God's perfect time for anything to happen. We started on a Tuesday night, which was the victory number or conclusion and I would soon see if my prayers were heard and answered.

The Dream

That night would not be like any other night. I found myself on a spiritual high. I hadn't been aware of all the numbers until then. The Lord brought to mind many things that night and the following Sunday morning. He had told me some things, like, "Don't get ahead of God. Wait on the Lord." I prayed and interceded for peoples, places, and events. The last time I'd looked at the clock, it was about 4:30 a.m.

The next thing I knew, I was having a vivid dream. I dreamed of going out to the garage and asking myself, "Why did I leave the lights on?" I noticed that all three cars were gone, and I asked myself if someone had stolen them. It was then shown to me that the tall and medium ladders were gone as well. However, the stepladder was still there. Also, the door keys to the house had been left in the door.

After the dream was over, I woke up. It was as if the Lord had said, "You must go to sleep to receive the dream, and then I will wake you to give you the interpretation." And that was exactly what He did. The interpretation was this: The lights being on meant that it was nighttime, and the cars would be gone for days and nights at a time. The two ladders were gone, symbolizing types of promotions, as my wife or I took another step up. The two missing ladders were medium and tall in length, which meant that I had already gone up both ladders. The stepladder was not needed, for I had already used it a long time ago. The keys left in the door appeared to refer to evangelization. Although we would be gone days and nights at a time, we would continue to come back to this address. The three (3) cars also was the conclusion of victory. I was not sure if the Lord was saying that we would be out of town, out of state, or out of country. When it comes to God, however, I believe that I should wait and see.

A Glorious House

David was *thirty (30)* years old when he began to reign for forty (40) years (2 Sam. 5:4). God always ascertains when we are fit and ready as he prepares us for His calling. The number *three (3)* in thirty is there for victory. Praise God.

On Tuesday morning, April 2, 2013, I had another dream from the Lord. This home that the Lord had been telling me about in my dreams was now visible as I stood inside of it, holding a broom in my hands. I remember asking myself, why was I not in my home? an excuse or a reality came to mind. As I stood there with broom in hand, I noticed that there was an overflow of water that wouldn't stop, as I talked and swept the water at the same time. Later I woke up and I noticed that this was not the home I lived in. The Lord had blessed my sweet wife and I with a nice home, but this was not a home to live in, for it was too glorious. It was something that would have come down from heaven. I had to be glorified before I could live in this awesome home. I believed this was to be God's grace and glory for me.

The Lord allowed me to only take a long look at the entryway and the large living room. The colors were earthy tones, so natural that they belonged in the state of Utah! This meant that this was the beginning of something. The water at the base of the doorway, which was the Holy Spirit, wouldn't go away (Zack. 4: 6).

It was Tuesday, the *third (3)* day, which was the victory number (Ex. 3:18). I had an appointment with my urologist, Dr. Becker, that morning to check my PSA. He came into the room and told me that my PSA was below *three (3)*. I responded by telling him that the Lord continued to assure me that I would be around for some time. He had given me the victory. Praise God.

The New Church

The new church that we had been going to for a short period of time had its services in high school gyms and facilities for a period of a little over *ten(10)* years, which is God's number of perfection and completion in the Bible. In one of his sermons, Pastor Vance revealed that he had been saved in 1989, which was the same year we had started to build our house. In 2012, which was God's government number, it had been exactly *twenty-three* (23) years, which I call my number. I had also heard the pastor use that number a few times as well.

On January (23) my number 2012, there was a countdown of *forty (40)* days, which was the number of probation, and Pastor Vance said he was frustrated that the church building would not open on time on March 3 and 4. The power was not going to be turned on until Tuesday, February 28. But God is a God of numbers. He opened the doors on March 10, 2012. Not only that, the doors were opened on the *seventh (7)* day of the week (God's number) on the *tenth (10)* of March, which was the perfect and complete day. And March was the *third (3)* month, which were the victory month! Those are shouting words! Hallelujah!

There was one more thing that is a fitting end to this story: the address of the church. The street address is 850 E. Cactus Avenue. The number *eight* (8) is the number of new beginning (Gen. 8:18; Rom. 6:4–5). The number *five (5)* is the number of grace (Gen. 15:9; Rev. 9:5–6). The numbers are there. One thing I learned is this: never try to make God's numbers work for you. And if you discover your own number, never make a decision just because your number is there. Let decisions be based on facts and good calculations. Leave the numbers up to the kingdom of God, and they will work themselves out. Otherwise, it is like trying to guess what God will do next. There have been times when I have seen my number show up, and I have gone for the bait. Those times remind me to just observe, stay focused, and never get ahead of God. It is a very exciting thing to see God's numbers work in our lives, for the Enemy cannot imitate God's fingerprints! To close this book out, it wouldn't be complete without pointing out the last month of the year. 2013 has been an exceptional year as well. As the Lord brought it to my attention, December this year starts out with a Sunday which is the first day of the week. Also, each day is lined up to prove my point of the numbers. Thursday I must point out that the first week is exceptional. We have double grace! Praise God. The second Sunday is the eight (8) day, the resurrection Sunday. Christmas closes out the last Wednesday the (25), which is the fourth (4) day and the fourth (4) week, the number of fourfold, the complete number of creation. And yes this calendar year and month would not be the same without Friday the 13th.We serve an amazing God.

God's Numbers

1 = A single member or individual of the same kind of quality. It can indicate God or man. (Eph. 4:5); one Lord, one faith, one baptism.

2 = "Witness" (John 8:17–18); Jesus said, "it is also written in your law, that the testimony of two (2) men is true. I am one that bear witness of myself and the Father that sent me beareth witness of me".
Revelation 11:3 And I will give power unto my two (2) witness.

3 = "Victory" (Luke 2:46); And it came to pass, that after three (3) days they found Him in the temple. (Matt. 20:19b) On the third day he will be raised to life. "Conclusion" (Jonah 1:17) Now the Lord had prepared a great fish to swallow up Jonah. And Jonah was in the belly of the fish for three (3) days and three (3) nights.

4 = "Fourfold" or "complete number of creation" (Gen.13;14) The Lord said to Abraham after Lot had left him, lift up your eyes from where you are and look north and south, east and west. (John 11:39)Then Jesus came, He found that he (Lazarus) had lain in the grave for four (4) days already. (Rev. 20:8) And shall go out to deceive the nations which are in the four (4) quarters of the earth. (Eze.1:10) each of them had four (4) faces

5 = "Grace" (Rev. 9:5a–6); And to them it was given that they should not kill them, but that they should be tormented five (5) months. And in those days shall men seek death and shall not find it; and shall desire to die, and death shall flee from them. (Gen. 15:9); And He said unto Abraham, "Take me a heifer of three years old, and a she goat of three years old, and a ram of three (3) years old, and a turtledove, and a young pigeon. The covenant is founded on grace, for five (5) living creatures are sacrificed to establish it.

6 = "Man" (Gen.1:26; 31); And God said, Let us make man in our image, after our likeness. Verse (31); and the evening and the morning were the sixth

day. Rev. 13:18); Here is wisdom. Let him who has understanding count the numbers of the beast: for "it is the number of man; and his number is Six (6) hundred threescore and six (6)

7 = "God" (Gen. 2:2); and on the seventh (7) day God ended his work which he had made; and he rested on the seventh (7) day.

8 = "Beginning" or "New beginning" (Mark 16:9a); Now when Jesus was risen early the first day of the week (Note: Count on the calendar from the first (1) day (Sunday) to eighth (8) day, (Sunday) would be the eighth day). "New Beginning," (Rom. 6:4–5); therefore we are buried with Him by baptism into death: as Christ was raised up from the dead by the glory of the Father, even so we also shall walk in newness of life. Verse (5); for if we have been planted together with Christ in the likeness of His death, we shall be also in the likeness of His resurrection. (Gen. 8:18); And Noah went forth, and his sons, and his wife, and his son's wives with him.

9 = "Gods fourfold (4) grace (5)," (Matt.27:45-46, 50); Now from the sixth hour there was darkness over all the land until the ninth (9) hour. Verse (46); And about the ninth (9) hour Jesus cried with a loud voice, saying, "Eli, Eli lama sabachthani? That is to say, My God, my God, why hast thou forsaken me?" (Note: In verse 45-46, we have nine (9) in both verses, Jesus being full of God's fourfold grace). Verse (50) Jesus

when He had cried again with a loud voice, yielded up the ghost. (Note: Verse 50, shows that He can now give us His grace and truth). Also, nine (9) is the number that much be split to the number (4), and the number five (5). (Rev 20:8) And shall go out to deceive the nations which are in the four (4) quarters of the earth. (Gen.15:9); The Lord said unto Abraham, "Take me a heifer, a she goat, and a ram all three years old and a turtledove and a young pigeon.

10 = "Completeness and perfection" (Gen. 8:5); And the waters deceased continually until the tenth (10) month: in the tenth (10) month the first day of the month, were the top of the mountains seen. (Luke 19:13); And He called his ten (10) servants, and delivered them ten (10) pounds, occupy till I come.

12 = "God's government" (Rev. 21:12); And had a wall great and high, and had twelve (12) gates, and at the gates, twelve (12) angels and names written thereon, which are the names of the twelve (12) tribes of the children of Israel. (Acts 16:25–26); and at midnight Paul and Silas prayed, and sang praises unto God: and the prisoners heard them. Verse (26) and suddenly there was a great earthquake, so that the foundations of the prison were shaken: and immediately all the doors were opened, and everyone bands were loosed.

13 = "God's hidden number of victory in the Bible" (Gen. 37:2); these are the generation of Jacob, Joseph, being

seventeen years old. (Gen. 41:46); And Joseph was 30 years old when he stood before Pharaoh, king of Egypt. (Note: Thirteen years between slavery to prime-minister). (Josh. 6:3-4); and you shall compass the city, all ye men of war, and go round about the city once. Thus shall thou do six (6) days. Verse (4) and seven priests shall bear before the ark seven trumpets of rams' horns: and the seventh (7) day you shall compass the city seven (7) times, and the priests shall blow with the trumpets.

21 = "The Trinity: God the Father, God the Son, and God the Holy Spirit" (Gen. 1:26); And God said, Let us make man in our image, and likeness.

23 = "My personal number. Separated, it is the number of witness and victory. Together they add up to "grace." (Rev 11:3a); And I will give power unto my two (2) witnesses. (Luke 2:46a); And it came to pass that after three (3) days they found him in the temple. (Gen. 15:9); The Lord said unto Abraham, take me a heifer, a she-goat and a ram all three years old, and a turtledove and a young pigeon.

40 = "Rest" (Judg. 3:11), and the land had rest for forty (40) years. "Probation" (Num. 14:33); And your children shall wander in the wilderness forty (40) years, and bear your whoredom, until your carcases be wasted in the wilderness.